ADVANCE PRAISE

"Matthew is an effective, dedicated, and benevolent executive who is building up his family's fourth-generation business to continue to grow and prosper. In Build to Flourish, he generously shares his lessons learned, from joining the company after a successful career outside of the family business through becoming president. Build to Flourish is a must-read for all executives, especially those working through generational leadership transfers."

—KARL WILLIAMS, CEO, WATERSTONE CONSULTING

"Matthew Powell is the real deal. He's a voracious reader, eager to learn, eminently coachable, and in the words of leadership genius Patrick Lencioni, 'humble, hungry, and smart.' So it's not surprising that Build to Flourish is no armchair leadership book. Matthew has been in the trenches—literally—and has written an accessible, savvy, and practical book with learnings for both aspiring and seasoned leaders."

—PHILIP C. BERGEY, SENIOR DESIGN PARTNER AND EXECUTIVE COACH, DESIGN GROUP INTERNATIONAL

"In the world of business valuation, succession, mergers, and acquisitions, almost all of the works are about the founder, the long-time CEO, and occasionally about a business partnership that worked. Insightful literature is rare for the successor who plays cleanup for anything left undone and whose perspective and wisdom must grow if they are even to grasp what needs cleaning. Matthew Powell opens a locked door and turns on the lights with this memoir about his long road as a successor. His is a much appreciated and already wise voice."

—MARK L. VINCENT, EXECUTIVE ADVISOR AND
FOUNDER, DESIGN GROUP INTERNATIONAL AND
THE SOCIETY FOR PROCESS CONSULTING

"Build to Flourish. What a lovely, transparent journey Matthew shares in entering a fourth-generation family business with its frustrations and challenges of stewardship. He goes through much historical and current management thinking, projecting it forward into the future. It is a worthwhile read for family-owned businesses, management, and leadership. He seeks the actualization of the total person, personally: family, community, physical, and spiritual—an excellent reflection for anyone seeking excellence. I look forward to the next chapter in this journey."

—RICHARD R. PIEPER SR, PAST CHAIRMAN OF
GREENLEAF CENTER FOR SERVANT LEADERSHIP
& CHAIRMAN EMERITUS PPC PARTNERS INC.

"Only a handful of family businesses have survived economic and business cycles with complex ownership dynamics through multiple generations. Matthew, the fourth-generation family leader of Century Fence, shares perspectives on honoring traditions while championing cultural and business stewardship for future generations."

—ERIC K. JORGENSEN, PRESIDENT &
CEO, JX ENTERPRISES INC.

BUILD TO FLOURISH

BUILD TO FLOURISH

Leading Your Family Business into the Next Generation

MATTHEW POWELL

BUILD TO FLOURISH
Leading Your Family Business into the Next Generation

FIRST EDITION

ISBN   978-1-5445-3779-5 *Hardcover*
        978-1-5445-3778-8 *Paperback*
        978-1-5445-3780-1 *Ebook*

To my Mom, I miss you.

CONTENTS

INTRODUCTION

PREFACE

WHAT DO PLANTS HAVE TO DO WITH BUSINESS?

As an optimist—and maybe even an idealist—I want to see organizations full of humans flourishing. What does that look like? I think the better question is: what does it feel like? Simon Sinek articulates flourishing best: an organization of humans that feel inspired at the beginning of the day, feel safe throughout the day, and feel fulfilled at the end of the day. Imagine how much better society would be if this was a reality for every parent going home to their families.

To better understand human flourishing, we need to understand how nature flourishes. For a plant to flourish, there are four main ingredients: air, soil, water, and sun. Every variety of plant requires a different quantity, timing, and magnitude of these ingredients, but they are, nonetheless, the ingredients. While seemingly simple, the growth, blossoming, and flourishing of a flower is intricate and nuanced. Every variety requires a different and specific amount of air, soil, water, and sun.

Just as a flower needs four main ingredients to flourish (air, soil, water, sun), the next-generation leader of the family business also needs four main ingredients to help the business and all of its people to flourish as well. Successfully leading and growing a family business requires the next-generation leader to do more than just turn a profit. It requires that leader to diligently work *with* the family, *in* the business, *on* the business, and *on* the self.

This book captures my mental model of family business and documents my thoughts and meditations as I actively progressed through the organization to become a fourth-generation president in the business, with my goal to help the business and all of our people flourish.

The mental model was constructed after many years of studying intensely, reading literally hundreds of books, conversing with best-in-class executive coaches, joining a CEO peer group, and networking with world-class leaders.

This book is not supposed to serve as a playbook but rather to provide tools (i.e., ingredients) for those who have embarked on the immensely fulfilling journey of carrying forward family business. Just as a cactus and a rose need different implementations to flourish, so does every family business—BUT it's still the same ingredients: air, soil, water, and sun for the plants; for the business, it's work with the family, in the business, on the business, and on the self.

A family business that can **do good** for the customer, **be good** for all stakeholders (employees, vendors, customers, community, and shareholders), and **do well** to prove it's possible to balance it all is a family business worth devoting one's life to.

The journey has sunny days, stormy days, peaks, and valleys. The landscape and journey of family business can be deeply enriching. I hope the pages in this book can provide assistance to building your family, your business, and your community toward attaining human flourishing.

Sincerely,

Matthew Powell

PS: If you would like my handwritten notes of my top ten most influential books in my transition to president, then please go to matthewpowell.com/buildtoflourish.

MY FAMILY BUSINESS DYNAMICS

THE ORIGIN STORY—THROUGH THE LENS OF G4

Without history, there is no context. Without context, there cannot be effective leadership. I did not grow up directly involved in the family business, but when I joined full-time, I became a student of Century Fence's journey and how it has prevailed for decades. Business is really about humans walking bravely through the marketplace seeking to provide a bargain to the customer while giving the team (i.e., employees) a safe, inspiring, and fulfilling environment to give their all for the goals of the organization.

The story of Century Fence starts well before my existence—even before my grandfather was born. It starts before The Great Depression and even before "The Great War." It starts in 1881, sixteen years after the Civil War.

HENRY BRYANT: FOUNDER—GENERATION ONE

"Success is never final. Failure is never fatal. It's courage that counts."

—JOHN WOODEN

Henry Bryant, my great-grandfather, was born sixteen years after the Civil War in 1881. He was born in Waukesha, Wisconsin. Henry took a longer-than-normal route to complete college. The longer-than-normal route helped him to appreciate the importance of an education. He ultimately received his degree from Cornell University in 1904. Once out of school, he decided to become engaged in the steel industry by working for the mammoth company, Bethlehem Steel, in Pennsylvania. Bethlehem Steel was essentially the "Amazon" of steel companies back in the early 1900s. Henry invested four years working on the East Coast and gained industry expertise, but he realized he was not cut out to climb the corporate ladder of a large company. He had an entrepreneurial itch to start his own venture.

Henry decided to head closer to his midwestern routes by starting a business just outside Chicago. He started a scrap metal business to leverage his steel expertise. Well, it did not go as planned, and he closed the business down. But, he got back up on his feet and started a second business. He started a vacuum cleaner sales agency. Well, it did not go as planned, and he closed the business down. He got back up on his feet and started a third business! It was a patented mail opening machine business. It also did not go as planned, and he closed that business down as well. Three consecutive failures in four years. At the age of thirty-two, his professional career consisted of four years in the steel industry on the East Coast and three failed businesses in Chicago. Yikes.

Despite the setbacks, Henry did not allow the failures to define him. He got back up on his feet and started his fourth endeavor in Wisconsin. He opened the doors in 1913 as "Henry Bryant &

Company." Henry was a much more seasoned business owner by this time and decided to make a second attempt at the steel industry with a scrap metal business. This time he was more aware of his blind spots, and he approached the business with eyes wide open.

In 1914, after about a year in business, Henry, who was a history buff, sensed war clouds brewing in Europe. Henry made a bold move with his insights of tension in Europe and entered into contracts with all of his scrap metal customers to buy their scraps for 10 percent above the market price for scrap metal. If steel was selling for $100, then Henry was offering $110. All of his customers were probably laughing when he offered the contracts.

Henry's parents were probably concerned too that he would be left with a fourth business failure. Henry remained committed to his thesis and business plan. He continued to sign customers to his generous offer of buying scraps 10 percent above the going rate.

Well, Henry's courageous patience finally paid off. In May of 1915, a German U-boat sank the British luxury liner Lusitania. This act of war created a huge spike in the price of steel, putting Henry's perceived ludicrous contracts into the category of genius. Henry profited over $100,000 in 1915, which is over two million dollars in twenty-first-century dollars.

ROBIN SHARMA STATES ABOUT
VISIONARIES: "EVERY VISIONARY IS
INITIALLY RIDICULED BEFORE REVERED."

This moment marked the start of many more business successes to come in Henry Bryant's career.

In 1917, Henry volunteered for the war and was commissioned to be in France. When he left for the war, he incorporated his business to protect his personal liability and promised his girlfriend, Margaret, that if he came back home alive, they would get married and start a family. About a year after he was stationed in France, the armistice was signed, and Henry came home. The good news was that he came home to marry the love of his life, but, unfortunately, he also came home to a board of directors seeking to dissolve Henry Bryant & Company. The directors believed the business was not worth anyone's time. The company only made $3,000 in profits in 1917, so the board suggested shutting the doors and moving on.

Henry rejected the resolution. He saw a bright future because he saw opportunity. The marketplace was transitioning from steam engines to diesel engines. Henry began buying outdated steam engine locomotives to extract all of the pipe from the machines. He took out the perforated and useless pipe within the locomotives, recast them to plug the holes, and painted them in aluminum paint to give them a shiny finish. He made the pipe as good as new to repurpose in the marketplace and sell as clothesline poles. Henry turned useless, perforated steam engine pipe into an everyday household staple. Once again, Henry had the courage to see beyond those around him because he had a vision.

In 1921, a couple of years after moving beyond just being a scrap yard, Henry decided to change the name of the business to Waukesha Steel Products. The company's position in the marketplace was ripe to capitalize on the strong economy of the roaring 1920s. Henry began dabbling in the fence industry, and it took hold with tremendous success. So much, in fact, that four years later, in 1925, he decided to change the name of the business again: Century Fence Company. The company continued to thrive throughout the 1920s, carving out a niche and a brand for itself as a fence contractor.

Good times do not last forever. The stock market crashed in 1929, and the country went into a deep, dark economic depression. Henry was in a predicament, just as every other business owner in the early 1930s. There was no business to be had. There was no oxygen in the room. Henry was determined to keep the business alive. With four children, a wife, and a dog at home, he mortgaged his home to keep the business afloat. He took on debt during the darkest days of the US economy in the hopes of providing for a brighter future when the economy resurrected.

The company survived the Great Depression and the shortages of steel during World War II, and it was poised to be part of the great infrastructure investment of the 1950s. Dwight Eisenhower signed into law the installation of a large infrastructure investment for the country. Century Fence was in a prime position to participate and contribute—it participated in the installation of guard rail, signs, and right-of-way fences.

Henry's optimism and hope for a brighter future and willingness to risk everything he had to keep his dream alive is the ultimate expression of courage. Through the trials of the early days, Henry instilled a hunger for more in the company's spirit. A foundation of grit to take on the most challenging of days, keep climbing, and never becoming complacent.

ANTHONY ("TONY") BRYANT: GENERATION TWO

"Without humility there can be no humanity."

—JOHN BUCHANON

Tony was born in the middle of The Great Depression as his father was wrestling with keeping the company alive. Tony was the youngest of the four siblings and grew up around the business. He would go into the shop as a kid sweeping the floors and tying gates. Tony was drawn to the game of capitalism at an early age, and through his involvement with his backyard victory garden in Waukesha, Wisconsin, he learned, at an early age, the importance of striking a fine balance of price for the customer.

Tony had a knack for numbers. With this innate talent, he pursued an MBA at Northwestern University. While Tony was getting his MBA, he completed his thesis on a profound concept that forever changed the trajectory of Century Fence. He helped put in place a profit-sharing plan to reward employees for their efforts. Tony inscribed into the DNA of the organization the concept that all members of the team, regardless of their placement in the hierarchy of the organizational chart, deserve the opportunity to be rewarded for their efforts as if they are an owner. Up to one-third of the profits were explicitly put aside for the team and then distributed. This type of thinking requires humility. Most people in a position to keep profits and squeeze will do just that. Tony instilled a humility into the spirit of the company that must always be preserved. Tony's vision to appreciate all members of the team is profound and forever ingrained in the organization.

Tony completed his master's and stayed involved on the board at Century Fence while he began his career at a bank in Chicago. After a couple years in Chicago, his father, Henry, called to ask him to join the business full time. The company was gaining success and needed more working capital to keep up with the increasing demands of the business. Tony agreed to join the business, take over the finance department, and speak the language of the bankers to secure a line of credit. Tony used his skills to help professionalize the operations to take it to a new level. Tony was ultimately elected to become president of Century Fence in 1964.

Tony stepped into the role as president at the age of thirty-four with a couple years of experience in banking and operational experience within the company, which excelled in the fence industry during his early years as president. While Tony was leading operations, he was also keeping his eye out for new business opportunities. He promoted a culture where new opportunities were never stifled but encouraged. In 1969, Vice President of Construction Joe Tanke brought a new idea to the table. The Wisconsin Department of Transportation (WISDOT) was putting out to bid road painting throughout the state of Wisconsin because the state did not want to self-perform the work anymore.

Tony and Joe reviewed the plans and threw a number at the project without any idea what the estimate should be. A couple days went by and the Century Fence team was eager to see how the results turned out so they could sharpen their pencil for future bids and be more educated about future road striping opportunities. Century Fence was the only bidder!

Tony and the Century Fence team had to scramble. They did

not have a truck. They did not have the paint. They did not have anyone who knew how to drive or install the project. Nonetheless, the team figured it out! A truck was found for sale in St. Louis, Missouri, and was brought up to the parking lot in Waukesha for the workers to figure out how to paint the roads. The journey to becoming the leader in the road striping industry started with no experience, in a parking lot figuring out how to get the job done.

Tony set the stage for getting into a new business by providing an environment for people to bring wild ideas to the table. Tony's humility to be open-minded allowed Joe Tanke to bring an idea to the table that has forever upgraded the trajectory of the company. Tony's humility to share the financial success with all teammates and his willingness to hear new ideas is in the spirit of Century Fence. As the current leader of the organization, my job is to ensure we foster and build upon Tony's humility.

In addition to Tony's humility, he has had tremendous patience during his career. He never pushed family into the business or put any pressure for family to get engaged. He had a vision to keep the business family-owned to ensure the right priorities remain intact. Tony has held the torch for two generations as the bearer of culture and ownership well into his nineties. Tony's patience is beautiful and an inspiration, allowing me the opportunity to realize the beauty of family business on my own.

MATTHEW POWELL: GENERATION FOUR

"Help employees become better versions of themselves, (and) the company will necessarily become a better version of itself."
—MATTHEW KELLY, DREAM MAKERS

I was born in 1989. My father's career landed my childhood on the East Coast in Charlottesville, Virginia. I grew up in a small college town where my dad's work as a doctor at the University of Virginia supported our family. It was a beautiful city to grow up in, and my parents provided a loving home for me to see the world through a lens of abundance and possibility.

I had the opportunity to witness a marriage and partnership of love, clarity, and hard work. My parents exemplified for me what service to family and community looks like. Jim Kwik states, "The greatest lessons you teach is the life you live." My parents gave me an incredible education without ever providing a syllabus or sitting me down for a formal lecture. This background of my upbringing is important because it shares the lens through which I ultimately learned to see business and will become apparent in the pages ahead.

My first exposure to the family business was when I was about seven years old, and my grandfather asked me if I wanted to get a tour of the facility. I was not interested, but he told me we could play Pac-Man when we returned from the tour. I said YES! I vaguely remember the tour, but I remember the excitement of getting back to my grandfather's house to play Pac-Man.

My next exposure to Century Fence was when I was finishing high school and realized I needed a job to make enough money to get a car. I could not come up with a high enough paying summer job to buy a car, so I called my grandfather in desperation. When I explained my situation to my grandfather, he calmly replied with a hint of enthusiasm, "Well, I have the antidote for you. Work on getting a flight up here after school, and I will work on getting you a position for the summer." I worked for the summer in the field, getting a deep appreciation for the work ethic required to be successful in the construction industry. The summer was a success because I was able to buy a 1996 Honda Civic with 200,000 miles two weeks before my first semester of college started!

The following summer, I came back to Wisconsin to work for the company again. I needed enough money to pay for insurance and gas to last my entire sophomore year. It was another great summer experience with the opportunity to appreciate the people who make the company a success.

I completed these two summer engagements without ever having the intention to join the family business full-time after college. I was going to make my own path. Construction was not the industry I wanted to be in. I wanted to be in finance. I completed my college degree and landed an investment banking position at SunTrust Robinson Humphrey in the mergers and acquisitions department. The time at the bank provided me with an incredible, practical finance education as a liberal arts major. It gave me the technical skills to properly analyze data and make informed decisions. Over the course of a year at the bank, I gradually became more intrigued with the prospects of joining the family business. I was starting to realize business is more than just the numbers on the spreadsheet that I can masterfully analyze.

I decided to write my grandfather a formal letter to express my interest and put my heartfelt aspiration into words. We connected and came to an agreement on my start date and everything that comes along with a full-time position. Once we finalized the details, I left my job at the bank, and then my high school sweetheart and I got married. After the wedding, we packed up the U-Haul and made the fourteen-hour trek to Wisconsin and landed in an apartment in downtown Milwaukee.

Once we got our U-Haul unpacked, I immediately started working. I jumped into the field, building relationships, asking more pointed questions, and seeking to understand processes throughout the organization. Throughout my first one and a half years in the business, I was simply listening and learning. I was documenting every department's processes to understand how the organization went from quoting a job to receiving cash for successfully completed projects and everything in between. I completed this project while also addressing safety and compliance issues, in addition to executing a refresh of the website for the company.

The following years of my transition were dedicated to understanding the business through stewarding a digital transformation all the way up to my promotion to president. It was certainly an emotional journey for everyone involved in the company to transform the business from typewriters (yes, typewriters!) to a digitally oriented company.

The years leading up to becoming president were infused with massive amounts of organizational change in all aspects of the business from people, software, hardware, etc. We have been actively adapting to the twenty-first-century landscape.

FAMILY OWNERSHIP STRUCTURE

Every family differs in how they are involved in their respective business. This is the basic upper-level structure of my family business. My operational engagement with family has been quite minimal with me seeking my grandfather's counsel over the years as chairman. This will hopefully provide context for the rest of the book.

G2: Matriarch and patriarch (my grandparents)

G3: Board involvement and shareholders, not involved in the day-to-day operations (my aunts)

G4: I am the sole representative of the fourth generation, and I am involved in all aspects of the business from operations, governance, and ownership.

FINDING MY FRAMEWORK

INTRODUCTION

Every first chair leader goes through a transition to reach that position in their respective organization. This book is a meditation of my journey and the lessons I've learned during it, within a framework of four key ingredients to achieve human flourishing in family business.

Prior to joining my family's construction business, my career choices were based on status, money, and prestige. My thought process was very typical of a college graduate, and my decision to join an investment bank was based upon those factors. As *New York Times* bestselling author Timothy Keller wrote in *Every Good Endeavor*, I was not making choices that took into "consideration...my gifts and passions to contribute to the world."

My first job out of college was working in mergers and acquisitions in an investment bank, and it provided me the opportunity to wear a tie every day to signal how important and smart I was. But I was also miserable. I was drowning out the callings of my heart. As Lee Hardy, professor of philosophy and urban studies once put it, "The ego wants you to choose a job and a life you can use as a magic wand to impress others." After spending over a year in investment banking, I decided to give my grandfather a call to see if there would be an opportunity to join the family business.

When I agreed to join the family business in 2014, I knew I was in for a big transition. To start, I took a 75 percent pay cut and eliminated all the false trappings of prestige I'd previously mistaken for success.

I had no idea the mental, emotional, and spiritual journey I was embarking on by making this choice. I was uprooting my fiancée at the time (now wife) from the East Coast to the Midwest. I was transitioning from finance to construction. I was going from a public company to a private company. I was leaving behind a built-in friend group at the investment bank, relocating to a city where I had no connections to people my age.

This was a life-changing event I could not fully appreciate. Since I came from a background in mergers and acquisitions, I thought of business in terms of EBITDA, EBITDA, and EBITDA (earnings before interest, taxes, depreciation, and amortization). Today, over seven years into my family business journey, I think of business as STEWARDSHIP.

For me, this marks a profound transition from a bottom-line focus to a much deeper appreciation for the drivers of profits: people, culture, organizational behavior, and leadership. I hope my seven-year journey to becoming president of my family's business will provide insights into the value of a focus on service and building systems of resilience.

I have found my journey of stewardship to be energizing rather than draining. If I had stuck with a pursuit based solely on bottom-line growth, I would have become bitter. I would not have sought a more holistic approach to self and organizational development. Embracing stewardship has allowed me to bring a deeper meaning to the family business and to my life's work.

Viewing things through a lens of stewardship is like watching a play with an appreciation for the beautiful music produced by the orchestra underneath the main stage. The orchestra is the underplay. Without the music, the play is not nearly as rich and meaningful. The play might even become boring, and you might want to leave. Imagine leading your family business without developing this appreciation for the underplay.

There's a reason most family businesses do not survive beyond the second generation. A garden requires attention driven by intentionality that it not be filled with weeds. Strengthening a family business such that it can sustain generations of succession, competition, technological innovation, and many more headwinds requires fertile soil. The dynamics of the family behind it must be able to balance power, love, and money.

Ego always tries to take root in this fertile soil and must be pulled out like the invasive weed it is for there to be space for genuine human flourishing. A mindset revolving around stewardship provides an energy of humility and service. Stewardship has the power to sow the seeds of sustainable success. Making a buck is not the hard part. Creating a resilient organization honoring the family, the employees, the customers, and the community is the true challenge.

How do we find clarity amidst the noise? This is the challenge for every leader. Creating alignment is the job of a steward.

I hope to offer you a look into the unique perspective of leading from the second chair in preparation to take on the first chair role. This book is about the journey of a fourth-generation family member finding his way in a family business.

By following my heart's calling to join my family's business, I've embarked upon a journey of truly discovering who I am and how I fit within an organization so much larger than myself. This experience of transitioning to president of the family business has set me on the path to becoming the best version of myself, one where I have integrated my whole self into an organization rich in over one hundred years of history and culture.

In the wise words of Ben Witherington, "Your work is your prayer."

THE TWO PHASES AND FOUR LAYERS OF A FAMILY BUSINESS

As a second chair leader, I experienced two distinct phases of my family's business. The first phase was experiential, like learning the landscape. The second was leadership and learning how to become effective within a complex and sometimes emotional system.

EXPERIENTIAL PHASE

I've experienced this business in four distinct yet interconnected layers, not unlike an onion. In order, they are:

1. WITH Family
2. IN Business
3. ON Business
4. ON Self

The experiential phase starts on the outside. During my tenure, I worked my way in. The act of joining the family business started with a letter which led to a phone call to my grandfather to negotiate my starting salary. With that settled, the next step was for my wife and me to relocate to Wisconsin so I could begin. I spent that first year deepening my relationships with my grandparents and aunts. We were new to Wisconsin and had lived hundreds of miles across the country from my grandparents and aunts for my entire childhood and early adulthood.

While deepening these relationships, I invested time with various departments in order to better understand not only our processes but the industry itself. My first year on the job was focused on working IN the business with a pen and paper always at the ready.

Once I became familiar with our processes, I was able to help improve them. I did this by working ON the business.

I reached the core of the experiential phase when I realized my broad-brush strokes of leadership required more nuance. At first, my style of leadership primarily focused on doing what was right for the organization. As a regrettable result, after only two years in the business, I hurt a young, talented employee, and she quit because of me. This was the pivotal point in my leadership journey. I hurt someone when my intention was to help. This made me realize as my influence and visibility in the business increased, the consequences of my actions were amplified. My experience in school did not prepare me for the complexity of organizational behavior and the nuance required to lead.

Not long after this epiphany, I asked to have lunch with a mentor of mine in order to ask for advice on how to prevent talented people from quitting because of me. It was a difficult and overwhelming moment to realize the authentic intent to help is not enough.

This marked a decisive turning point for me. I began to appreciate the true power of self as I transitioned into my next phase of development: the leadership phase.

Figure 1
Experiential Phase: Wandered into these distinct layers of my time in the business until I stumbled into the importance of the core, ON Self.
2014: WITH Family—joining business
2014/2015: IN Business
2016/2017: ON Business
2017: ON Self

This journey began in 2017, when I invested in an executive coach to guide me on this journey of leadership. I have been on an intentional journey of leadership growth ever since. I have cultivated relationships with executives, owners, coaches, and mentors, and I have invested time in CEO peer groups.

The leadership journey is not completely chronological because I'm constantly learning and developing executive skills within all four of the same layers found in the Experiential Phase. However, if I could offer any restructuring, it would look like the exact opposite of the prior order:

1. ON Self
2. ON Business
3. IN Business
4. WITH Family

Starting from a place of self-leadership deep within my core, I found myself steadily working my way *back to the outside,* where I began my journey in 2014. Accordingly, this book is split into those same four sections, detailing the lessons I've learned from all the amazing people in my life, the resources I have stumbled upon, and the perspectives I've gained. In 2021, I grew from a newlywed to a newly minted father, and by the end of the same year, I finally took a seat in my company's first chair.

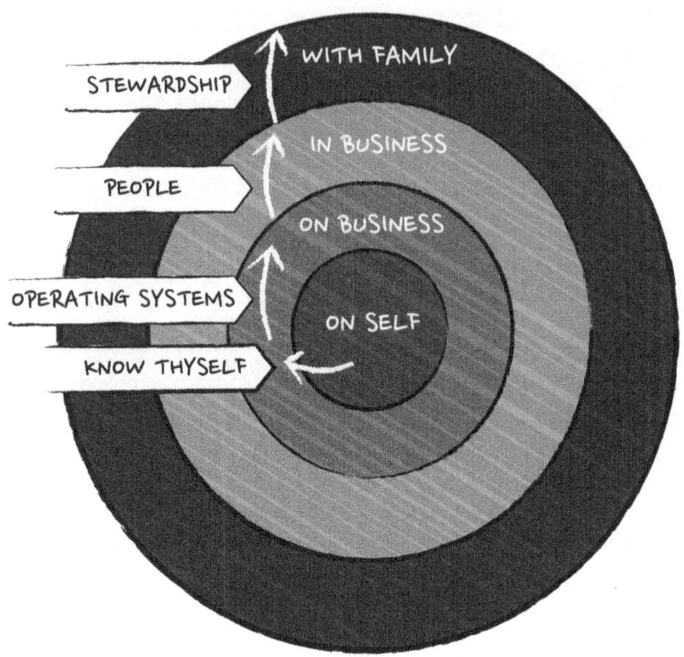

Figure 2
Working through the leadership experience and touching each of these layers
intentionally and on a journey of continuous improvement.
2017/2018: ON Self
2018/2019: ON Business
2019/2020: IN Business
2021/2022: WITH Family

FINDING A FRAMEWORK THROUGH EXPERIENCE

Each distinct layer along this journey of stewardship requires
intentionality and love. All four layers are important because
stewardship is a process of discovery, one where we must learn
how to create an environment where all humans can flourish.
During my seven years in the second chair, I personally peeled
back these layers to investigate and learn. As a result, I discovered a world of enrichment unknown to me before.

Experience has indeed taught me the proper journey for any leader starts from within, at one's core, gradually working outward. That said, every layer is important.

ON SELF:

"Knowing yourself is the beginning of all wisdom."

—ARISTOTLE

A dear mentor of mine shared some advice that really resonated when I hit a point of fatigue in my transition. It couldn't have come at a better time: I was experiencing a period of frustration during my second chair experience. He told me, "So goes you...so goes the rest of your organization."

If you are stale, then the company becomes stale. The company needs us to serve from a full cup, not from a place of exhaustion. An effective steward is also one who is well in tune with their own hardwiring. Self-awareness is a superpower. We must understand our weaknesses, strengths, prejudices, and preferred forms of communication. An appreciation for one's wiring helps us develop the ability to steward an organization into a state that sustains generational flourishing.

ON BUSINESS:

"We don't rise to the level of our goals; we fall to the level of our systems."

—JAMES CLEAR

Working on the business is where an executive begins to make a mark. Systems run the business, and people run the systems. An astute leader is fine-tuning the systems and the team.

If we envision working in a business as, say, laboring on an assembly line, then the act of stepping away and walking up to the balcony overhead is working on the business. This requires intentionality. Many leaders and owners may never consider this layer or find enough stillness to realize it exists. Working on the business is an act of humility, understanding we have to be willing to sit in the uncertainty and the unknown. The company's overall vitality and resilience depend upon leadership building future value ahead of the current operations.

IN BUSINESS:

"Vision without execution is hallucination."

—THOMAS EDISON

This part may seem self-evident. A business needs to have operations and cash flow. All businesses need to execute. If there is no operational excellence, then there is no oxygen. Without the success of day-to-day operations, everything else is not possible. Leaders are with the people. Being engaged in the day-to-day is a sign of a leader who cares. Understanding the people working on the "assembly line"—whatever your actual industry may be—is a given. This is the ability to work on the "smarts" of the business. This is a focus on the technical, which includes understanding marketing, sales, logistics, job cost, finance, and more. A leader who shows competence and benevolence builds trust. Having a pulse on the day-to-day operations is a baseline skill to build that foundation of trust with the organization.

WITH FAMILY:

"In an infinite game, the primary objective is to keep playing, to perpetuate the game."

—SIMON SINEK

Family and business are infinite. There is no time horizon, and there is no finish line. There's no such thing as coming in first in relationships or even coming in first in business. Strong relationships help the family business to transcend generations. The success of a family business, in my eyes, is continuing the legacy and staying in the game.

This framework has helped me successfully complete my transition to the role of president and continues to serve me as I steward my family business forward. I hope you will find value in the journey I have documented in these pages. We will start at our core, focusing on ourselves, and then we will work our way out, back to where the journey started—with family.

PART ONE

ON SELF: SELF-LEADERSHIP

CHAPTER ONE

"You are the greatest project you will ever work on."

—JIM KWIK

During a mountain hike in the spring of 2019, my wife and I witnessed an eagle soaring through the cloudless, blue sky. The majestic creature hardly moved its wings as it glided gracefully with the currents. The eagle spotted a tree, swooped down, and flawlessly landed on a branch. The great bird was perched a hundred feet high on the tree, gazing over the landscape with an air of calmness and quiet confidence.

Why was he confident? Was it because of the size of the massive tree? Was it because the branch he'd landed on was so sturdy?

No. The eagle was confident because he was truly aware of his own abilities. This self-awareness allows creatures like eagles to move through life with perfectly fluctuating degrees of peace and strength.

Today, the world is in dire need of eagles.

Satya Nadella, CEO of Microsoft, once said, "The more you

know yourself, the better prepared you will be for a changing, difficult world." Becoming a stoic eagle starts with immense effort and attention toward self-development. A leader's journey of growth starts with looking inward and working on oneself every day.

The act of leadership is an act of learning. I have come to appreciate it is my job to grow. It is my job to learn and seek out education. It is my job to unlock the secrets to success by tapping into the power of books, mentors, and *listening*.

The growth of an organization is dictated by the growth of its leaders. Strong leaders accept full responsibility for their company's culture and results. As Johnsonville CEO Ralph Stayer put it in *Flight of the Buffalo*, "My organization reflects my leadership behavior."

Once we have begun the journey of self-leadership, we can begin cultivating leadership within others. Pursuing the leadership of others without first developing a strong sense of self-leadership is like attempting to train athletes while personally suffering from obesity.

Mother culture and status quo are powerful undercurrents, yet life is shallow when it isn't fueled by intention. The world can quickly become a small echo chamber without the intentionality of self-leadership. Life is short and passes by if one does not water their seeds of greatness.

Right now, at this moment, we are exactly where we should be. We are exactly where we are because of the choices we have made and the habits and routines we have molded.

LEADERSHIP 101

Leadership is an art. The only way to work on your business is through leadership. The most successful leadership of others is found in and after the development of self-leadership. Only once we have begun the journey of self can we truly begin to help and serve others.

To that end, the best definition of leadership I have ever come across is from business advisor Jim Collins:

> Leadership is the art of getting people to want to do what must be done.

It is essential to have clarity of self in order to understand what must be done. Then, we lead others into alignment to proceed.

This understanding is key. As Robert Greenleaf described in his 2015 pamphlet, *The Servant as Leader,* "Anybody could lead perfect people—if there were any." We are fallen people living in an imperfect world. If human beings were perfect, there wouldn't be a need for leadership.

UPGRADE FROM 1.0 TO 2.0

When it comes to computers, software upgrades can provide critical support. Similarly, it is imperative to upgrade oneself. Growth provides momentum and enrichment.

We must sharpen the axe so we might be able to make a deep impact in the lives of others. It is essential for leaders to seek growth and to chase dreams. Dreams are at the core of our existence. We must live out and master the journey of the chase. We must constantly be evolving into our next version of self.

There's an old saying, "If you do what you've always done, you'll get what you've always gotten." This is true. Companies grow with people. Simple. So, how can you guide a company if you are not growing as well?

A powerful example of the importance of self-leadership can be found by studying Apple co-founder Steve Jobs. "Jobs 1.0" launched a successful company and brought an amazing product to market. However, one doesn't have to look far to find unhappy stories of Jobs's leadership at the time. He was very abrasive and even combative at times. Ultimately, Jobs was even ousted from his own company when the board voted to relieve him in 1985.

Undeterred, Jobs continued his personal path of growth. Twelve years later, Apple brought him back as CEO. However, this time he was "Jobs 2.0." After over a decade of work and self-evaluation, the "new" Jobs was a much better leader, championing his company and lighting the way forward for Apple. Under his renewed stewardship, Apple redefined technology and became a great, enduring company that crossed multiple industries, including mobile devices, music, TV, computers, and more.

During my seven years in the second chair, I upgraded myself multiple times. I believe I have gone from Matt 1.0 to Matt 1.1, Matt 1.2, and onward. Stepping into the role of president required that I master a new skillset. The journey and its result completed my upgrade to Matt 2.0.

Of course, Matt 3.0 is next.

This is so important because in order to expect other people to grow, a leader must set an example and grow first. Accordingly, Matt Powell 2.0 has leaned into the following skills:

- Hire great people and integrate them into a cohesive team
- Prioritize culture
- Hire for values and temperament
- Know how, when, and when not to delegate
- Hold unit leaders accountable for keeping culture vibrant
- Make wise decisions for long-term greatness
- Stay calm and mitigate the impulse to take control when things go wrong
- Confront existential threats by moving outside of the company to mentors—not inward

My primary responsibility as a leader is to catalyze a clear and shared vision for the company. Not only do I assist in creating that vision but I will become masterful at consistently communicating it. Leaders who lack a definite vision are like compassless captains who steer their ships into stormy seas.

KNOW YOUR "WHY"

Understanding my purpose gives me a stronger threshold for dealing with the tough days. A clear and defined "why" provides us with an unwavering compass. A strong purpose that underscores our personal values provides depth.

My values and purpose help me get up on those cold mornings when I just "don't feel like it."

MY VALUES:

- **Wonder:** Appreciating and posturing to explore God's creation
- **Adventure:** Exploring the world locally and globally
- **Growth:** Tapping into my divine potential and helping others tap into theirs
- **Love:** Cultivating compassion, kindness, deep conversation, and meaningful relationships
- **Service:** Contributing to the wellness and success of others

My mission is to build people and institutions of human flourishing.

My values (behavior) and my mission (purpose) provide the clarity I need in order to withstand large obstacles and, as I already mentioned, the ability to push through difficult days. It isn't logical to count on blue, sunny skies every day.

Teams want to follow leaders who have clarity of purpose. In this area, most companies are average; most leaders are average. Great companies have leaders with an unwavering, thoughtful, and clear purpose. Building a great company starts with determining truthfully why you, as a leader, get out of bed every morning. What motivates you? It needs to be more than just making a profit. Saying the reason you get out of bed is just to make money is a lot like saying, "I'm getting out of bed to breathe."

I have found it very helpful to seek stillness and to give myself the space to think bigger—to think deeper. Now, as president, I am able to see the positive results from the efforts I went through to plant these seeds of change. I have needed to rely on the strength of their roots now that I have stepped into this powerful leadership role and inbound requests for my time have continued to increase.

BEING MINDFUL OF THE INVISIBLE PROGRAMMING

There are beliefs that our environment, such as friends, family, and even society itself help to cultivate. This invisible programming helps craft our subconscious view of the world. The lens in which we view ourselves directly affects the messages we tell ourselves about our situation, life, and future. Some people refer to these scripts as "inner chatter," "monkey mind," or "lizard brain."

No matter the name, it is important to recognize this reality in order to confront the powerful limits invisible programming inspires us to place upon ourselves. When triggered, our subconscious belief about a certain topic spawns an internal conversation. That, in turn, presents us with an opinion of ourselves and an assessment of potential opportunities. In positive cases, this leads to accomplishments and results.

CONFIDENCE

Dealing with the day-to-day operations of a family business in transition is emotionally exhausting and, understandably, many fail. Those in power don't always transition gracefully. Without having confidence in myself, I could easily break and say, "I quit!"

Confidence cultivates resilience. Without confidence, we are fragile; we are a twig. There are many hurricane seasons in a family business transition. They come and go, sometimes between the sudden howls of tornadoes. As mindful leaders, it is imperative that we try to remain like a blade of grass during these storms: flexible but firmly rooted to the ground.

I have experienced so many moments where I've felt misunderstood, underappreciated, and unaffirmed. Without cultivating confidence, one can break.

Self-reflection has revealed that, for me, the emotion of anger can rapidly suck up my confidence, inspiring my lizard brain to consume my thoughts with fear. This only serves to further prove to me that the maintenance of one's mindset is imperative for leaders. We often do not learn about the significance of mindset or the importance of confidence in school, so this is one area where we must seek support elsewhere.

I remember feeling a lot of anger regarding issues I experienced during my transition to president. Whenever the emotion bubbled up, I found I was too focused on what other people thought. That drained and redirected my energy away from my family and away from becoming the servant-leader and steward I intended to be. Anger brought me down. I was meant to play at a higher level, so it was important for me to try to look at what was angering me from another angle: feeling anger is an opportunity to learn how to fly above the turbulence.

Confidence can serve us, making us as resilient as a blade of grass in a hurricane. Taking on the role as an upcoming leader in a family business puts you in a situation of being the symbol of change in all levels of the organization: operational leadership, board leadership, and family leadership. This amount of change can create fear and uncertainty while everyone in all levels of the organization is experiencing a transition.

Where there is a lot of fear and uncertainty, there is a lot of potential pain. By being confident in myself, I brought a new-found sense of energy to the business. The trajectory is set. I'm here to serve. I'm here to live my greatness. Those who are suffering from change will not impede my personal growth.

SELF-CARE IS *NOT* SELFISH

As leaders, we must be diligent in service to ourselves. We cannot properly serve others from an empty cup. We must serve with a full cup. Human flourishing cannot be achieved without the leader living up to and leaning into their own potential. A stale leader will wind up leading a stale company.

Self-care is not optional. Self-care is mandatory. This vital practice incorporates all aspects of the human experience: physical, mental, emotional, and spiritual.

Here's another way to look at it: you must secure your own oxygen mask before helping others retrieve theirs. It's not about being selfish. It's about serving from one's God-given potential, and sometimes that means focusing on ourselves.

CHAPTER TWO

If you fight for your limitations, then you get to keep them. When my daughter was fifteen months old, she didn't think twice about standing up again after she fell. She did not believe in limits. She didn't even know what they were, so she got up and kept trying. Every time she fell, she got back up with a smile on her face. She had an instinctive growth mindset, and though she constantly fell, she fell forward, improving and growing every day.

This brings me to an inspirational, cautionary tale shared by Anthony de Mello in his book, *Awareness*:

A man found an eagle's egg and put it in a nest of a barnyard hen. The eaglet hatched with the brood of chicks and grew up with them.

All his life the eagle did what the barnyard chicks did, thinking he was a barnyard chicken. He scratched the earth for worms and insects. He clucked and cackled. And he would thrash his wings and fly a few feet into the air.

Years passed and the eagle grew very old. One day he saw a

magnificent bird above him in the cloudless sky. It glided in graceful majesty among the powerful wind currents, with scarcely a beat of its strong golden wings.

The old eagle looked up in awe. "Who's that?" He asked.

"That's the eagle, the king of the birds," said his neighbor. "He belongs to the sky. We belong to the earth—we're chickens." So the eagle lived and died a chicken, for that's what he thought he was.

We are all golden eagles. Mother culture and the notion of "normal" pushes us down toward the flightless barnyard chicken. We must always seek to rise above, and a powerful way to accomplish this is with a personal, intentional investment in self-leadership.

Limits are learned. Whoever you spend time with, you become. Self-leadership is the act of waking up to our innate, God-given greatness and becoming mindful of the impact of our words, actions, thoughts, character, and habits. We must cultivate a state of growth in our inner chatter. On the outside, it's important to set an example of growth as we seek to increase the competency, capacity, and abilities of our team.

There are three main ingredients to increasing the boundaries of our limitations:

- Visualization
- Habits
- Mindset

In the same way a rose garden requires constant care and attention, so too does the inner chatter of our mind. The lizard brain (fear) can become very powerful if not put in its place. Behavior is driven by belief.

Again, limits are learned. Don't fight to be a chicken when you are meant to fly free.

GRATITUDE IS THE ANTIDOTE

"If you focus on what you lack…you lose what you have. If you focus on what you have, you gain what you lack."

—GREG MCKEOWN

Life is suffering. There are so many reasons to be upset; there are so many reasons to be miserable. Life, like business, has so many ups and downs—a journey of problem after problem. There is little wonder why families and institutions are in need of grounded leaders.

I have found gratitude to be the antidote to the negatives life throws my way. Gratitude helps reframe life as happening "for" me rather than "to" me. Gratitude flips the script from "victim" to "victor" and transforms a brittle, fixed mindset into a resilient growth mindset. A daily practice of gratitude nourishes the soil for beautiful blossoms while eradicating the pesky weeds.

IMPORTANCE OF SUFFERING

No challenge, no change. It is during the struggle where growth occurs. A routine with constant challenges leads to a life of deep connection, deep work, and deep thought. As Seneca the

Younger described, "You have passed through life without an opponent....No one can ever know what you are capable of, not even you." A lack of hardship creates apathy, and an easy journey without hardship leads to an unfulfilled, hard life.

My transition to president was infused with massive dips, frustrations, and disappointments. At the time, I questioned the pain. I felt it was not fair, and I should have been treated differently and guided differently.

As Henry Longfellow put it, "Into every life...some rain must fall." Even now from my position in the first chair, I know there will certainly be more rain in the years to come—and this is true for the leader of any company. I am grateful for the challenges I've faced to date because I have begun to test, learn, and stretch my capacity for facing struggle. I have built muscle to face this type of resistance. As Ryan Holiday wrote in *Courage is Calling*, "Iron sharpens iron, resistance builds muscle."

Consider John D. Rockefeller's reflections on the challenges he faced as well: "Oh, how blessed young men are who have to struggle for a foundation and beginning in life....I shall never cease to be grateful for the three and half years of apprenticeship and the difficulties to be overcome, all along the way."

All of the challenges I've faced seasoned me for the first chair position. The pain and disappointment was an incredible teacher for becoming the leader I am today. Without challenges and suffering, I would not have sought mentors, wisdom, or personal growth at such breakneck velocity. Suffering required me to ramp up my personal growth to weather the storm—the storm which, all along, was training me for leadership.

KNOWLEDGE IS PROFIT

I find solace remembering how Rockefeller built his empire. He went against the common thoughts of his peers and became a knowledge worker before it was "cool." Rockefeller leaned into moments of stillness to manufacture ideas for growth.

Few people in the nineteenth century used their brains for work. According to economist Robert Gordon, in the 1870s, 46 percent of jobs were in agriculture and 45 percent of jobs were in crafts or manufacturing. Work was only considered "work" if it was visible and tangible. As Morgan Housel explained in *The Psychology of Money*, "Rockefeller's job wasn't to drill wells, load trains, or move barrels. It was to think and make good decisions."

As a leader, my job is to be an observer of the outside world so I can absorb what's useful and bring new ideas to the table. My job is to make good decisions. My job is to think because today, knowledge is profit. The economy has evolved from the industrial age into the information age.

HIGHEST AND BEST USE

When living in a world that overvalues struggling in the weeds, it is important to remember the true role of the executive. We must understand the various ways we can add value within the organization.

In *Linchpin*, bestselling author Seth Godin expressed a hierarchy of value with the following chain:

**Create/Invent > Connect > Sell >
Produce > Grow > Hunt > Lift**

All levels of this value chain are critical, and it's important for the leaders to infuse meaning into each role.

I found it is crucial for the leader of the organization to be disciplined enough that they have time to be in the higher level activities of creation and connection. The activities lower down the chain are more urgent and can easily steal our attention from the deep work of creation and invention.

SEEKING COUNSEL

Harry Truman was in a difficult situation with General Douglas MacArthur. MacArthur was an absolute legend but he was jeopardizing world peace with his actions and insubordination in Korea. He was instigating a larger world war with mainland China while Truman hoped to find peace.

MacArthur was jeopardizing the role of the president of the United States by actively undermining Truman's actions. Truman's issues with MacArthur had been building for many months and years, but he was afraid to address the issue head-on because MacArthur had so much clout. His legacy was well-known among the military and a large population of the US. Eventually, MacArthur overstepped his bounds so much that Truman had to take action.

He knew whatever his decision there would be an uproar.

Instead of simply leaning on his own understanding, the president brought together four highly distinguished generals—including General George Marshall—to receive their counsel. As they discussed the situation, the men came to a unanimous decision: to release General MacArthur from his duties.

As soon as the decision became public, all hell broke loose. Congress and the media went off the deep end, personally attacking Truman for this choice. The media hammered Truman, focusing on all the great things MacArthur accomplished during WWII without any discussion of MacArthur's present-day threat to world peace. Whipped into a frenzy, people wanted Truman impeached for such an embarrassment of a decision.

Multi-day hearings were held over Truman's decisions to release MacArthur. Fortunately, Truman's process of seeking counsel proved his decision to be a fundamentally sound one. The hearings began with Truman on the defensive. However, Truman's wise preparation began to shine here. MacArthur needed to backpedal on his egregious actions and the threat he posed to national security during his time in Korea. Truman and his four councilmen were instrumental in communicating the logical and careful decision they made as a group to release MacArthur.

Seeking counsel requires awareness and humility. Seeking counsel also takes a significant amount of time to invest in relationships that are worth leaning on for highly important decisions. As the next leader in my family business, I could not afford to learn on my own. I needed to leverage the wisdom of those who walked the path of executive leadership before me.

I used my youth to my advantage. I sought to serve those on my left and right and embarked on this journey with my fellow teammates. With my promotion, the concept of unilateral decision-making became a leadership model of the past.

What's more, I tapped into knowledge at all levels of expertise in the company. Just as Harry Truman leaned on his generals for the tough decision to relieve MacArthur, I leaned—and continue to lean—on my teams for their wisdom. Even today, I continue to build trust with them so they are always open to having deep, meaningful conversations. Artificial harmony is absolutely toxic for leaders hoping to tap into the power of the people.

This service model is where I found my strength, just as Truman found his. He and his generals enjoyed a mutual respect for one another because Truman always sought to serve them, and they served him when he was vulnerable. Seeking counsel is imperative when tough decisions are to be made, and it falls to the leader to call those shots. If a leader is not making tough decisions, then they probably aren't needed and they certainly aren't leading. That's the point of leaders: to make tough decisions not everyone will like. A leader is not a friend. A leader makes decisions for a better future, fully appreciating and enduring the pain of the moment.

Truman did not have an easy run in his career in politics. He was dismissed by Franklin Roosevelt despite supporting him fully throughout the New Deal era, and he was poor throughout the first forty-plus years of his life. Truman was unwavering in his commitment to the principles of fairness and justice. He was a very determined individual who was willing to ride the waves in order to chase his higher goals of serving his community and country. Throughout the early part of his career,

Truman was backstabbed repeatedly by various people but he never sought revenge. He would continue to move forward, putting his ego aside in service to focusing on larger goals.

While he was running for his second term as senator, Truman was so broke that he was sleeping in his car because he could not afford a hotel room. Still, he kept his head down and kept showing up.

As I seek to build my reputation, I want to build a similar resiliency as Harry Truman. I want to remain focused on the first principles and not allow the circumstances around me to dictate my trajectory. I endeavor to show up every day and put my ego aside.

In my previous role as vice president, it was important for me to continue to strengthen my skillset as a leader. I experienced many lessons in quieting my ego while leading underneath the president who came before me. It was easy for me to get frustrated and play the victim card, like, "He doesn't get it," or "Gosh, I can't do anything until he retires…"

However, it is the job of the second chair to bring ideas and initiatives to the table even while they are not in charge. These ideas must be clear and sound within the context of how the company has been led up to that point. Even though the president at the time didn't have a computer or email, it didn't mean I could not prepare the rest of the company for the future. It was my job to set the stage for the future growth of the company with humility, and even today, as president, that is still my job.

Harry Truman is a great leader to learn from. He was a servant-leader—earning his stripes through serving others—and he never backed down from a challenge. Even in his personal life, Truman chased after Bess, his future wife, wholeheartedly. He was a meager farm boy chasing after a beautiful lady with plenty of suitors, but he out-hustled everyone. He wouldn't take "no" for an answer, and he continued to show up for Bess day after day and year after year.

Truman's humble beginnings granted him an eye for focusing on those who were less represented. He also saw the value of being as frugal as possible with taxpayer money. He did not engage with corruption while seeking funding and building the infrastructure for his represented county. He went out of state to find banks with favorable interest rates, and he found contractors who would build roads at a fair price.

Instead of getting snuggly with all the politicians in his town, the future president truly served his community. His unshakable refusal to stoop to corruption made him some powerful enemies, and as a result, Truman experienced many disappointments in his career. However, he never lost sight of his larger trajectory and, ultimately, he became president of the United States.

CHAPTER THREE

"You are the average of the five people you spend the most time with."

—JIM ROHN

I would not be where I am today without the network I intentionally cultivated. Your network is your real net worth. Just as the old saying goes, "It takes a village to raise a child," it takes a network to grow a family business in the twenty-first century.

I admired my grandfather's network and how he seemed to know everyone in Wisconsin. During his time as the president of our family business, he was always "in the room where it happens."

My network turned into an invaluable compass, capable of pointing me in the right direction over the years. My network has helped me build lifelong friendships, it has paved the way to meaningful conversations with mentors, it has allowed me to better engage with coaches, and it has given me the opportunity to absorb intelligent insights from others. All of these things elevated my ability to lead my family business into the twenty-first century.

Networking can be daunting. Accordingly, I prepared myself to attract talented people into my circle. First, I took a lot of time to build a story to elevate my presence. I was very intentional about how I scripted this. I used to think being humble and downplaying my role was always the right thing to do. My wife helped me realize I can represent myself with confidence while not being cocky. There is a difference between being assertive and being aggressive. It's my responsibility to properly signal this line as a leader of the family business.

I've spent time building and investing in relationships through sending emails and letters, setting coffee dates, and planning happy hours. Over the seven years I was vice president, I built a track record of positive outcomes for the family business. As a result, I have been able to string that into a storyline I share with people I meet.

I've been very selective in who I invest my time with and who I divulge information to. Competent and benevolent mentors are such invaluable assets on the journey of growing into the role of president. Mentors in my life helped expedite my executive skills, network, and point out blind spots on the journey.

Your network broadens your horizon and is a catalyst for personal and professional growth. It's important to build a network of people who are diverse and smarter than you. Also, surrounding oneself with people who are better than you and over-indexed in other aspects of life is enriching. If you are the smartest person in the room, then you are in the wrong room.

THE POWER OF PATIENCE

Jesus is not only a spiritual figure, he is also a great example of a leader who charged forward with a vision and built an enduring institution. His presence on earth has literally defined time: Before Christ, BC, and Anno Domini, AD. Jesus is the epitome of an effective executive, and there are numerous lessons to learn from him. As an aspiring, effective executive, Jesus's ability to institutionalize a vision in his thirties is a tremendous accomplishment. There is much to learn by studying his journey, his approach, and his life.

Imagine having unlimited abilities and insights yet *taking it slow*. Jesus's approach demonstrates significant wisdom and encourages us to infuse patience into our leadership style. Others have adopted this same approach. For example, Bill Hewlett and Dave Packard of HP have said, "Don't grow too fast. You need to grow slow enough to develop good management." Even the US military has a saying on the subject: "Go slow to go fast."

At a young age, Jesus was extraordinarily patient with his disciples and in his mission work. His timing was perfect. He never rushed his mission work, and he never gave up on his disciples when their faith wavered. Jesus allowed the slow drip of his miracles to permeate and become symbols of hope. Jesus had the patience for his stories and his good works to be absorbed by his disciples so they could carry on the vision even when Jesus was not physically present. A typical, ambitious thirty-something looking to change the world would burn the candle at both ends, looking to fix as much as possible and as fast as possible and never losing a moment to spare. A typical thirty-something with such abilities would not have had the patience to accept the wavering faith of a teammate, like Peter in the storm.

Throughout my transition—and now as president—I sought to be mindful and not interject too quickly. Over the years, while learning the organization, I have had many opinions about how the company should operate and actions I believed the company needed to take in the future, but all of that had to be filtered first through patience. I am not going to get anywhere by jumping in with guns blazing, forcing my views onto anyone.

Patience is an extraordinary asset for young, aspiring executives. Every time I ask for patience, I'm given opportunities to practice it. Patience allows for relations to prevail over being right and alleviates ego. It is an essential ingredient to building a great, enduring company.

Succession involves the development and growth of the aspiring executive while also balancing the needs and sense of loss from the outgoing executive. When the outgoing executive has not fully accepted their departure or is not otherwise well diversified in life, they can struggle to step away. The upcoming executive must practice patience daily. Prior to assuming my role as president, I was required to exercise patience on a daily basis. I had to allow the culture and systems of twenty-plus years to continue. I had to learn that I do not need to "fix" everything. I do not need to infuse my ego into the company's culture and systems.

Jesus saw brokenness everywhere, from the culture to the systems of society. He exercised patience in his approach. He did not make it all about him. He strategically picked his moments and sought to foster the development of his team (i.e., disciples). He carefully bent the culture rather than snapping it into strict alignment.

Patience is a rare commodity and a muscle worth strengthening. Today, I am able to look back on the years of this succession process as a time I did not allow my ego to dictate my actions.

RECIPE OF FORESIGHT

"In every moment of time, historian, contemporary analyst, and prophet—not three separate roles. This is what practicing leadership is, every day of life."

—ROBERT GREENLEAF

A primary benefit of having a leader is the ability to rely on their foresight. Leaders are only able to provide foresight when they understand the past, value the present, and appreciate the future. These three distinct vantage points create the recipe of foresight, and a great leader can seamlessly jump between them.

1. The Historian: past
2. The Contemporary Analyst: present
3. The Prophet: future

HISTORIAN—THE PAST PROVIDES CONTEXT AND INSIGHTS

A 105-year-old company has deep cultural roots. I was only able to *begin* to provide effective change in the organization after wearing the historian hat for at least a year. It was important that I learn to appreciate the context of the business. In order to facilitate meaningful change, I've come to realize I need to understand the hesitancy behind "This is how we've always done it…" By having a true understanding and knowledge of the company's processes, I'm able to empathize with the loss of old processes. Change can be scary for people, so it is my job to slowly, carefully, and patiently begin pointing a light toward the bright side. Becoming a historian of the family business is helping me to build trust.

Being an "absorber" of history at a micro and macro level is becoming increasingly important to me as I grow into my role. The view from this type of rearview mirror begins to build a database where leaders can build out a thoughtful thesis for the future.

CONTEMPORARY ANALYST—THE HERE AND NOW

Being truly present in the moment is a skill. Time traveling is a constant battle for me. Being present in a conversation, debate, or meeting is imperative for making effective decisions in the moment. An executive is in charge of making decisions and resolving bottlenecks. Understanding the complexities and the current processes is a must. One cannot live in Future Land or be plopped on the historical Island of Irrelevance while there's a fire burning now.

PROPHET—VISIONS FOR THE FUTURE

The future performance of the team and company is ultimately where a leader makes a living. A leader's ability to articulate their visions and goals for the future is of the utmost importance, but this cannot be done without carefully examining the past and present. An effective leader is able to share and articulate their vision in a "sticky" fashion that resonates with the rest of the team.

Too often, sloppy, unclear communication is the default. Everyone gets lost working in the business without anyone stepping on the balcony to ensure the team is heading in the right direction. A clear message puts a leader and the team on the hook for results. Jesus, Moses, and Mohammed were pretty darn clear in how they communicated their visions! There's a reason Jesus taught with parables and aphorisms—that is to say, he kept it simple with one-liners.

Foresight is where value is created by a leader. An executive who only has awareness of either the past or the present can quickly become an overpaid administrator or technician. An executive living solely in the future is all fluff.

Some of the techniques and routines I'm building into my daily practice include:

- **Historian:** past
  - Reviewing the history of the company with my grandfather
  - Constant conversations with employees about the past
- **Contemporary Analyst:** present
  - Weekly engagements with employees to get a pulse
  - Meditation and journaling
- **Prophet:** future
  - Spending creative time in the morning reading a good

book and writing thoughts down about the company and the future

Building a sustainable, daily rhythm that incorporates all three proper vantage points is one of the ways I strengthen my leadership skills.

SUCCESSION AS A STOIC

Succession is painful. It's messy because it can feel like an experience of loss for those who are transitioning out. My journey positioned me such that I watched this unfold in full force. Longstanding family businesses experience transitioning of operations, boards, and ownership.

The succession process is much more difficult than I would have ever imagined. It is a pinch on both the operations and the ownership—my family—because everyone is wrestling with their respective next chapters. This situation required deploying some of the strategies first outlined by stoic philosophers of the past. For instance:

- Start small
- Work for the common good
- Don't be naive
- Get informed
- Be willing to change your mind
- Find allies
- Communicate

START SMALL

I had very little power during my transition, so I needed to focus on what I could control. I could build hope for the future by building relational equity. That said, small steps are no small thing. I needed to maintain this perspective and always move forward. Momentum for a brighter future cannot be understated.

WORK FOR THE COMMON GOOD

I could not make the transition about me. It was important to focus outward on what was best for the company and the team.

DON'T BE NAIVE

After seven years of noticing actions and patterns from my position in the second chair, I learned I should not expect anything different from what I'd experienced since Day One. When I was not included or involved in decisions, I had to learn to not be surprised. When I got shut down or when I was told an investment was considered a cost, I had to train myself to not be taken aback. A leader locked into a fixed mindset is static. Their thought process was not evolving, so I didn't need to be surprised. The status quo is predictable, and that's what I could expect.

GET INFORMED

Leaders are readers. My time in the second chair gave me ample opportunity to prepare and sharpen my metaphorical axe for the future when my time would become more taxed. When you're leading from the second chair, there is no need to waste any time. This is the perfect time to prepare and hone the craft of leadership. As a second-chair leader, I had the time to understand and study history, business, people, and myself.

BE WILLING TO CHANGE YOUR MIND

This transition taught me that it's important to be willing to adjust my thinking. The closer I got to assuming the president role, the more sure of this I became. This is not flip-flopping. This is growth and evolution.

FIND ALLIES

It's important to have people in my corner to vent to and also to seek their advice and benefit from their perspective. I'm always building alliances. When it finally became my turn to lead from the first chair, I had the trust and network to make positive change happen.

COMMUNICATE

Near the end of my transition out of the second chair, communication had narrowed to a one-way street. Nevertheless, I had to set an example for the workplace communication I wanted to see under my leadership. I learned the value of communicating to the team and of giving affirmations—particularly to those who hadn't ever received any. A good leader must set the tone of clear communication and, more importantly, listening.

CHAPTER FOUR

"Occupy the space you are designed to be in. Not too small. Not too big."

—ANONYMOUS

This definition of humility is liberating. We must give ourselves permission to fully occupy the space we are designed to hold. Go for it!

TOO SMALL—FEAR

We cannot maximize our full potential when we are stuck living too small. I know I am living too small when I allow fear (i.e., inner chatter) to dictate my actions. It is essential to dance with fear. We will never eliminate fear from our lives or careers, but we can learn to face it head-on. We do not have to allow fear to consume the space we are designed for.

TOO BIG—EGO

By living too big, we might be thinking too highly of ourselves. The ego is the enemy and always needs to remain in check. It's more valuable to cultivate perspective and awareness of our place in the world.

We are divinely made for greatness. Live into it!

THE TRIO OF PURSUITS

There are three core, individual pursuits I've come to appreciate in my daily life:

1. Truth
2. Health
3. Wealth

TRUTH—WISDOM

The pursuit of truth keeps me in a state of learning, and I've distilled for myself a recipe for a life well lived. Now, I deeply appreciate the importance of cultivating meaningful relationships and meaningful work. Life is meant to be shared, and it is best lived when we are in a position to be helpful and serve others.

HEALTH—YOUR BODY IS A TEMPLE

If the body and brain are not optimized, then everything about life decays. Our number one job is to keep our body healthy. Without health, there is nothing. Period.

A lot of people start having issues in their mid to late fifties because they sacrificed their health in their younger years. I strive to intentionally build habits in my thirties to ensure

I have good mobility, strength, and mental clarity for my journey later in life. I do not want to be stuck in rehabilitation mode in my fifties, sixties, and beyond. I want to be climbing mountains, running, and living in nature like we were designed to.

WEALTH—FINANCIAL INDEPENDENCE

Wealth is an imperative pursuit because it permits independence. It allows us to be who we truly want to be. If I'm not financially independent, then I'm susceptible to manipulation. Financial independence allows us to work on the most meaningful projects with the utmost integrity.

DIGITAL HYGIENE

"Don't pick up the phone every time it rings. It is there for your convenience, not the convenience of others."

—ROBIN SHARMA

Technology is a horrible master and a helpful servant. If technology is not strategically managed, then it becomes the biggest hindrance to meaningful, deep work. When used properly, technology is like a forklift. Productivity spikes. When technology is not used properly, chaos ensues. Specifically, the leader loses control of time, productivity, and deep work.

I'm constantly trying to reconfigure my relationship with technology. It requires constant tweaking because it is easy to cultivate bad habits with devices. I seek to be very mindful of my relationship with technology because it can lead me down a path of feeling unfulfilled. The distraction it offers pulls me away from adding true value to my family business, and it hinders my relationships (specifically with my family).

In our current era of "breaking news," the few leaders who choose not to be distracted by momentary trends can find themselves with a competitive advantage by seeking deep work with lasting impact.

Were he in the twenty-first century, Napoleon would have been a digital minimalist. He used to wait over a week to open his mail because he figured if something was truly a problem, he could step in after seven days to help resolve it.

The default settings of technology turn executives into administrative assistants:

- Email becomes instant messenger.
- Social media becomes your source of news.
- Solitude becomes non-existent.
- Deep work becomes a rarity.
- Interaction with employees, customers, vendors, and shareholders becomes shallow.
- Creating future value for your company becomes a dream rather than a reality.
- The executive becomes burnt out.

My technology best practices (on a good day I follow this strictly):

- Silence all call notifications from unknown numbers.
- Batch text messaging and do not have notifications.

- Schedule intentional meetings weekly with an agenda to reduce the ad hoc meetings.
- Check email twice per day insofar as non-emergency messages.
- If there is an emergency, everyone needs to be aware they can call me on my cell phone.

When it comes to digesting local, national, and global news, I don't want anything from social media. It's a complete waste. I should only use social media for creating content to share with others. Don't scroll for updates in the world. Allsides.com can provide information from literally all sides: left, right, and center. I am subscribed to Morning Brew for updates to my inbox.

Outside of work, it is important to unplug. I have not yet implemented it but plan on implementing "airplane mode" on the weekends.

A typical day with default technology is a day full of context switching and dopamine hits. All those dings and red notifications let you know how important you are to the environment where you spend most of your day. Default technology settings lead to shallow activities.

As a leader, it's important to empower your team to be able to make decisions based on principles. The team must understand how their leader uses technology so they might be inspired to apply similar strategies for their respective roles and context in the business.

I define a day's work as "well done" when it includes meaningful work and meaningful connections. I hold life to the same standard. Technology, if not handled strategically, hinders the most beautiful aspects of life and work: meaningful relationships and meaningful work.

VISIONARY EAGLE, FOCUSED FROG

Our family construction business has had non-family executives lead the business for over three decades who have risen through the ranks, so they provided leadership with unrivaled industry and marketplace expertise.

As an outsider to the family business—and as someone with a very different skillset—I've needed to find a new way to lead. The leadership of my family business was in the trenches for over two decades. These leaders have been "focused frogs." In other words, they have been extraordinarily specialized.

I, on the other hand, am not specialized. Consequently, I endeavor to fly above the operations, swooping into a department to implement a systemic improvement before necessity moves me to the next upgrade. I naturally jumped into this role, and this was a good thing. This business was in desperate need of a leader who could climb out of the mud, someone who could see beyond catching flies (profits).

In this era, being an eagle is essential. It entails flying above the verticals in the organization to find the intersections of technology expertise, industry expertise, people needs, marketplace needs, and most importantly, future changes. Breadth provides insights and growth. Specialization is good, but it creates a narrow focus.

Playing the eagle role felt very awkward initially. I was not sure if I was really providing value because everyone else was in the mud. I flew up above, identifying changes that had not been imagined in the company. Nevertheless, from the start, I forged ahead despite not yet being in the first chair. Why? Because it needed to be done.

In the 1960s, Nintendo was a Japanese playing card company. Gumpei Yokoi, fourth generation, knew the company needed to evolve. Yokoi became president of the company at the ripe age of twenty-two and began seeking new ways for the company to serve the marketplace. They failed a couple of times when trying to break into the food business. They ultimately landed in the entertainment tech industry. Yokoi was an expert at flying above the vertical of tech, connecting the dots, and finding the right people to execute his vision precisely in the intersections he spotted. Yokoi successfully transformed his company from an analog card-playing company into the Nintendo company leading the charge throughout the 1980s and 1990s.

Both birds and frogs are needed in business. One cannot survive without the other. When both roles are embraced, human *and* corporate flourishing can be reached.

EMBRACE THE COCOON

The butterfly is the epitome of a beautiful transformation. A caterpillar goes into a cocoon and then breaks out of its dark shell as a beautiful butterfly flying gracefully through the air. Time spent in the dark cocoon is uncomfortable. The cocoon requires a different relationship with struggle. The struggle and the effort to transform has a direct correlation to attaining results.

No effort, no results.

Throughout this transition, whenever I felt like my wings were clipped, I needed to remember the lesson of the butterfly: this is part of the process. Struggle is part of the process. I needed to build strength from within my cocoon in order to fully transform. It wasn't easy, but any great accomplishment requires great effort. This was no different.

I remember how depressed, stressed, and low I felt about eight weeks out from becoming president. At the time, I chose to reframe my experience instead of wallowing in it. I had been in that cocoon for over seven years. Even today, I deeply appreciate how this was the time to embrace the suck. I wanted to be rid of my cocoon, but the time I was spending there served to make me a stronger version of myself. I couldn't break free yet, not while I was still in a system where I felt cramped and unable to spread my wings.

But the cocoon made me stronger—so much stronger—and it empowered me to become acutely aware of my strengths and my shortcomings in a way I wasn't before.

We have to put in the effort to get the results. I had to invest time, sweat, and tears into this metaphorical cocoon. Now, looking back, I am grateful. The day I stepped into my role as president, I finally took to the sky.

Embrace the cocoon!

BUILDING DAILY RITUALS

The transition was exhausting. It came down to energy management. It was extraordinarily difficult to be expected to take on such an important job while not being given any latitude to operate outside the norms of the current regime.

This energy-sucking situation was the biggest test of my patience and morale. I found great solace by building in activities that are energy-producing to counterbalance this.

- Creating: writing
- Learning: reading
- Moving: working out

These staple activities have become an essential part of my daily routine. I maintain them now, even from the first chair. While the transition was difficult and depleted my energy, those core activities gave me significant energy and improved my leadership capacity. They helped me to be a better person and leader.

FAITH, FAMILY, FRIENDS

John Wooden is one of my heroes because he was one of the best teachers of life and basketball. He was a principled man. Wooden used first principles in his journey to self-mastery. Faith, family, and friends are the "Three F's" John Wooden invested heavily in on his path to self-mastery.

FAITH

"Spirituality is not about manifesting what you want, it is about manifesting what you are."

—WAYNE DYER

My faith has swung across the spectrum throughout my life. I've had seasons in my life where I lived with immense doubt in a higher power. Today, as a father witnessing the daily wonder of my first child, I find immense peace and hope knowing God is omniscient and omnipotent. Living in such a secular world, I find great solace in maintaining a daily, morning practice to water the seeds of my faith.

FAMILY

"LOVE…is best spelled T-I-M-E."

—NEIL STRAUSS

As a newly minted father, I love being fully present for ALL the special moments. The first time she talks, the first time she crawls, the first time she stands, the first time she eats. The little things *are* the big moments. This holds true for the rest of my family. For instance, I cherish the moments when I get to speak and break bread with my grandparents. I've been able to spend quality time with my in-laws recently, too, as they visited. It was so nice to be able to host them and to share this new chapter of life with them.

Life must always include family. The bookends of life, birth and death, only include family. Our first impressions and last impressions of life must be intentionally watered.

FRIENDS

"The dynamic of friendship is almost always underestimated as a constant force in human life: a diminishing circle of friends is the first terrible diagnostic of a life in deep trouble: of overwork, of too much emphasis on a professional identity, of forgetting who will be there when our armored personalities run into the inevitable natural disasters and vulnerabilities found in even the most average existence....But no matter the medicinal virtues of being a true friend or sustaining a long close relationship with another, the ultimate touchstone of friendship is not improvement, neither of the other nor of the self; the ultimate touchstone is witness, the privilege of having been seen by someone and the equal privilege of being granted the sight of the essence of another, to have walked with them and to have believed in them, and sometimes just to have accompanied them for however brief a span, on a journey impossible to accomplish alone."

—DAVID WHYTE

Friendship plays a big factor in one's personal depth and professional accomplishments. Life is too short to allow friendship to be determined by others. Friendship is like a garden that must be pruned and watered. The soil must be constantly evaluated and cultivated to foster opportunities for unique experiences and deep conversation. Friends do not need to stay the same. They can and should evolve as you evolve.

KNOW THYSELF

"If you don't stand for something, you will fall for anything."

—ALEXANDER HAMILTON

Knowing thyself is the first step toward building a resilient organization.

A leader must know who they are before leading an institution into the unknown. A leader cannot afford to be a cork in the ocean bobbing up and down with the opinions of the day. Instead, they must be like a lighthouse, grounded solidly to the shore and shrewdly looking out into the foggy unknown.

A leader must also be unabashed, capable of understanding their strengths, and willing to fully accept responsibility as they shepherd their company into the unknown. A leader must know what to say "yes" to while maintaining the ability to say "no" to everything that pulls focus.

To be the pioneer of the unknown, operational decision-making must be pushed downstream through the organizational chart. It is not a luxury; it is essential. It's the leader's job to lead the company into the uncharted forest of the future. It's the management team's job to run the company—to run and operate the *known*. Operational decision-making, like working in the business, is one of the biggest distractions to truly leading an organization forward.

THOMAS JEFFERSON—THE BAYONET GENERAL

As one of the authors of the Declaration of Independence, Thomas Jefferson was given every opportunity to take on an important, operational role in the Revolutionary War. He turned them all down because he knew who he was and what his strengths were. Jefferson went to his home in Virginia and began writing a new system of law while his fellow countrymen fought for their freedom.

During that time, Jefferson wrote 150 statutes, and fifty of them became law. The most notable among them, of course, was the separation of church and state. Jefferson said "no" to being the hero of the day because he knew he was more valuable building the finish line. The end of the Revolutionary War marked the foundation of a new beginning. The founding of America would have been haphazard, to say the least, if it wasn't for Jefferson's willingness to get ahead of the team. He had to say "no" to the war in order to say "yes" to do the deep work required to build a lasting legal system.

ABRAHAM LINCOLN—THE RAIL SPLITTER

In Abraham Lincoln's youth, he was frequently referred to as "lazy" because he did not enjoy or value the manual labor aspects of farm life. According to William Lee Miller, Lincoln was a "very lazy man. He was always reading, scribbling, writing, ciphering... He only showed industry in the attainment of knowledge."

Lincoln's skills with an axe were lackluster, but his thirst for knowledge was unquenchable. Everyone in the town knew Lincoln did not fit in. He was an odd duck. Lincoln even referred to himself later in life as a "strange, penniless, friendless, uneducated boy working on a flatboat for ten dollars a month." Lincoln's routes in the Midwest did not steer him from his passion for self-education, politics, and mastering the power of the written word. He was preparing himself at a young age to bear the burden of keeping the union together during the darkest of days. If Lincoln had not understood himself—if he had allowed himself to be swayed by the opinions of those in his town—he might have been a rail splitter his entire life. We might have never heard his Gettysburg Address. We might have never had a leader with the nuance, courage, and wisdom to guide the country toward a society free of slavery.

The United States of America is unequivocally improved from Lincoln's legacy because of the man's acute awareness of his strengths and his unwavering courage to live his life his way.

The United States of America would not exist as a thriving light of capitalism if Thomas Jefferson and Abraham Lincoln were not courageous, self-aware leaders willing to step into their strengths.

FRAMEWORKS FOR KNOWING THYSELF

Along this leg of the journey, I have found success in using these five personality frameworks to better understand myself:

1. The Core Values Index
2. Enneagram
3. Four Tendencies
4. DiSC
5. The Working Genius

These frameworks have initiated really great conversation and reflection for me to understand how to engage with the world and those around me.

CHAPTER FIVE

If knowledge is power, then reading is a superpower!

Reading is an expansive activity. It is a common trait of incredible people throughout history. One of the reasons Abraham Lincoln was considered lazy in his youth was because he spent so much time in the library.

Reading is an opportunity to collect and absorb wisdom from the brightest humans to ever walk the earth.

The educational system we experience today was originally created during the industrial revolution to create compliant factory workers. I grew up with the following, constant narrative: "Will this be on the test?" What a useless question.

I became a reader after college. It has changed my life. Here are my favorite quotes about the power of reading:

1. "If you haven't read hundreds of books...you're functionally illiterate."—General James Mattis
2. "To live the best life...you should have conversations with the dead."—The Oracle told Zeno

3. "A reader lives a thousand lives before he dies. The man who never reads lives only one."—George R.R. Martin

4. "The more that you read, the more things you will know. The more that you learn, the more places you'll go."—Dr. Seuss

5. "Not all readers are leaders but all leaders are readers."—Harry Truman

6. "If you don't read, you're not any better than people who can't read."—Mark Twain

7. "People [slaves, soldiers, and civil rights activists] died so I could have the ability to read."—George Raveling

8. "You could try to pound your head against the wall and think of original ideas or you can cheat by reading them in books."—Patrick Collison

9. "You are what you eat and you are what you read."—Neil Pasricha

10. "Fools say they learn by experience. I prefer to profit by others' experience."—Otto von Bismarck

11. "Reading is the nourishment that lets you do interesting work."—Jennifer Egan

For most adults, the tank is filled in one's early twenties and then drained until retirement. The sad reality is most adults live their lives functionally illiterate. This can be seen as a competitive advantage for those of us willing to invest in books.

We live in a digital world of constant change. We cannot expect to thrive in this world figuring it out on our own. Books have the ability to serve as a compass and North Star in all facets of life. Reading can even serve as one of the few analog moments in life. It is one of the few places where we are not swept into an algorithm of manipulation.

The brain is a collector of inputs and drives thoughts. Our inputs dictate our thoughts. Why not cultivate the soil of the brain with fertilizer, like the nutritious information it can find in books?

FORMULA FOR ACHIEVEMENTS

Inputs → Thoughts → Actions → Results → Achievements

The act of reading waters the soil of achievements. It's the opportunity to tap into the wisdom and suggestions of those who have come before us. With it, we are empowered to sharpen the tools to sculpt the granite sculpture of our life.

Reading is one of the few activities where we control the pace. We control the inbound, well-crafted, thoughtful message feeding the soul. The intentionality and strategic placement of prose elevate one's thinking and communication skills.

The act of reading waters the seeds of deeper, more impactful work—both your own and the author's. Not only does this increase our capacity to live deeply and effectively, it also allows us to live more than one life!

The journey to becoming a reader is simple: keep showing up, that will feel good, and then you'll crave it.

I realize now that throughout my childhood, I had blinders on. My days in school were spent seeking an "A" on every test. I was a high-status mule focused on one question when presented with new information: "Will this be on the test?" I wanted to know how to digest the information that resonated with the professor and on their terms. This reality is unavoidable for so many. Peter Drucker's management sentiment rings true for the educational system as well: "What gets measured gets done." The race to secure a high GPA disengaged me from the *genuine* pursuit of knowledge. As an adult, reading has become the vessel of experiencing a true education.

LEVITY AND GRAVITY

It's crucial to find a balance between positivity and negativity. Naturally, I find myself defining frustrations as personal, permanent, and pervasive.

In reality, these negative situations are temporary and specific.

Nothing is permanent. I was engaged in my leadership transition for many years. All aspiring leaders must embrace this as an ephemeral process. A lot of difficult processes tend to leave us focusing on gravity when, really, we would be better served by intentionally pointing our energy toward *levity*. There is so much good to be filtered through the angst of a transition.

We can all find ourselves struggling psychologically and drowning in negativity from time to time. It is imperative to find ways to inject positivity into a process that does not have intentionality. Building intentionality into a haphazard transition immediately makes it feel less chaotic.

The levity comes from reading, writing, networking, and taking care of ourselves physically.

The gravity—negative experiences—needs to be framed into the learning experience it actually is. Flops, otherwise known as difficult situations, present us with opportunities to strengthen into the leaders we want to become. The best leaders put gravity to work for them.

Finding comfort and contentment within the mix of experiences is essential for an executive. We need to appreciate what can be controlled and what cannot be controlled. Understanding how to respond to the external factors life and business throw at us is an important life skill.

Life happens *for* us, not *to* us.

ENERGY MANAGEMENT

Running on an empty tank is not sustainable. Mother culture has indoctrinated us into believing we should be addicted to exhaustion. However, hard work is not a linear function to output. Your company will not double in size if you double your time at the office. We must find ways to conserve energy and schedule activities that give us energy. It isn't wise or healthy to only fill our schedule with energy-depleting activities.

Winston Churchill held the weight of the world on his shoulders during WWII. How did he do it? Well, he was a master of conserving energy and also scheduled leisure time. On the conservation of energy, Churchill once said, "Never stand up when you can sit down, and never sit down when you can lie down."

Churchill had many hobbies. He was a man of leisure. Churchill would go to his lake house to lay bricks and paint. He produced thousands of paintings, and he wrote books. These activities helped him find clarity in his thoughts and understanding of the world.

If we don't control our calendar, others will. Even as the second chair leader of the family business, I began incorporating a ritual of scheduling daily activities I could invest in, all of which give me energy.

Each day, I try to incorporate:

1. Movement: an investment in the physical pillar
2. Reading: an investment in the mental pillar
3. Writing: an investment in the mental pillar
4. Journaling: an investment in the spiritual pillar

We need to cultivate the daily activities that fuel our tanks. Life is about the journey, and we don't need to experience it running on fumes.

POWER BECOMES BLINDING

It is important to build systems—along with inner fortitude—where leadership can receive candid feedback. I have witnessed firsthand the consequences of leadership without a learning environment—it creates a highly political and suffocating environment where others are unable to grow and become the best version of themselves.

It's important to acknowledge power and realize the intoxicating effect it can have, consciously or subconsciously.

Cultivating an environment of humility and eagerness to listen and learn is a great antidote to positional power.

The mechanisms I have put into place to make sure I do not become blind to power are:

- **Reading:** I drink deeply from thoughtful authors.
- **Coaching:** I have multiple coaches who provide different perspectives and make sure I'm growing alongside my increasing responsibilities.
- **Peer group:** I am always seeking to be in an intentional conversation with other leaders.
- **Educational trips:** It's important to always bolster my industry knowledge and stay fresh.

Leaning toward education and embracing a spirit of curiosity is a great antidote for subduing the ego.

BE WHERE YOUR FEET ARE

It's very easy to relive negative experiences. We do this by imagining them ahead of time and then time traveling to the past to suffer through them all over again. Life is hard enough—we don't need to endure our negative experiences more than once.

Being in the present is so critical. When you are at home with your family, *be* at home with your family. When we are at work and afraid of running into pushback, we need to schedule the meeting anyway. Don't push it off for hours, days, or even weeks.

Address it.

Be where your feet are.

This, too, is a superpower.

CHAPTER SIX

The sacrament of marriage does not live in isolation. Getting married was the best move I could have made for my career. Marriage is integral to professional life.

In 2013, billionaire philanthropist Robert Jepson visited my senior year leadership class. He founded the University of Richmond's Leadership School—the same institution I graduated from. I asked him why he was known for having the "golden touch" in business.

Jepson simply pointed to his wife and said, "It's her."

I thought it was a lousy answer at the time, and I felt like he didn't take my question seriously. I wanted a profound explanation of the formula for raking in billions of dollars. I wanted to hear about the leadership approach he finds most helpful in the boardroom. Instead, the billionaire gestured toward his wife, and she smiled, playing it off with humility.

I know now, Jepson was absolutely right.

Chelsea, my wife, has always been an amazing supporter of my personal and professional goals. Jepson and I are not alone in discovering this. For instance, Winston Churchill's wife was amazingly supportive. In *Clementine*, the prime minister's own chief of staff commented:

> [Clementine's] continuing confidence in Winston throughout their lives was his "mainstay." He firmly believed that without her, the "history of Winston Churchill and of the world would have been a very different story." Winston Churchill...took his strength..."from Clemmie."

Winston's wife was his foundation, and she was always by his side. She supported him during the dark days, providing great feedback and advice on how Churchill could improve his leadership. In fact, Clementine insisted that her husband become a better public speaker and, to that end, she would help him train. She believed he needed to become a better leader by tapping into inspiration rather than submission.

While Clementine's level of involvement in her husband's professional career was amazing, unfortunately, it appears her love and support were mostly a one-way street. *Clementine* goes on to state, "Even when she was in Britain, she spent little time with her children. Winston demanded more of her attention than they did—and got it."

Mary, Churchill's daughter, claimed, "Father always came First, Second, and Third." The prime minister's three kids accumulated a combined total of eight marriages, so it doesn't seem like the flow of love and attention was properly balanced.

Winston Churchill gave a lot to his country but took a lot from his family.

This, I never want to do.

Chelsea and I have been married for almost a decade. In that time, we have become great supporters of each other. We are partners helping each other achieve our dreams. I believe it's much more of a two-way street, and it is vital that love and support flow in both directions. We not only support one another, we solidify healthy habits together. For example, we have begun journaling every morning. We watch very little television, and we have mastered the art of turning our bedroom into a genuine sanctuary that can give us the best sleep.

We also consult with each other. Every morning and evening, we think critically about our goals, strategies, and tactics. We build each other up, ensuring we're focused on the long term. Further, we don't just dream together, we also vent, leaning on one another in times of frustration.

Today, I know when Robert Jepson answered my question all those years ago, he had, in fact, taken the question very seriously.

THE MAGIC OF EMPATHY

"Compassion is always, at its most authentic, about a shift from the cramped world of self-preoccupation into a more expansive place of fellowship."

—GREGORY BOYLE

In its simplest form, an organization is a group of people trying to do something together. Empathy is yet another superpower for a leader. A leader can never have too much empathy, and even the act of pursuing it is humbling. An effective leader must understand other people and their perceptions.

As Tich Nhat states, "Compassion is a verb." We must actively cultivate empathy with all subsets of people who drive the business forward. They are, in this order:

1. Employees
2. Customers
3. Vendors
4. Shareholders

The answers to all problems are found within the team. A truly empathetic leader must be nuanced enough in this area to tease out the answers. Then, it falls to the leader to apply those solutions at the strategic and systems levels.

Empathy is often developed through scars, wounds, and suffering. To be human is to suffer, and hardships offer us the opportunity to build this muscle.

Satya Nadella, CEO of Microsoft and author of *Hit Refresh*, explains that "only through living life's ups and downs can you develop empathy." In essence, suffering gives empathy a purpose. Suffering, when framed properly, can make us better leaders and can help us build up our empathetic superpowers.

Empathy is a core component I want to incorporate into the

stewardship of my family business. I see it distributed across three distinct levels:

1. Operations: digital transformation
2. Executive Leadership: succession
3. Ownership: mortality

All three levels present their own respective challenges. On the operational front, empathy is required in order to facilitate the company's difficult transition into the digital world. All change starts with a shedding of the old, and this is not without natural growing pains. It was important for me to feel my team's pain and to appreciate the value of doing things the old way before I could begin to create a different future. Throughout the operational transformation, I needed to gain a keen understanding of subject matter terminology and how the old system worked; I also needed to be capable of providing better solutions in newer systems.

In short, leading a company into a process of change when nothing had been changed for over two decades was an uphill battle.

On the leadership front, I needed to put myself in the shoes of a leader who had dedicated his life to the family business, one whose entire identity was deeply entwined in the business. I needed to imagine his sense of loss and provide him the space to grieve in his own way.

Again, *Hit Refresh* offers wisdom on this topic: "An empathetic leader needs to be out in the world, meeting people where they live and seeing how...[business] affects their daily activities. No product or policy works if it fails to reflect and honor the lives and realities of people."

Business is about how we make people feel. It's that simple—and that hard.

IMPORTANCE OF SABBATH

God designed us to have a day of rest. No machine can redline forever. No leader can redline forever, either. We are designed for hard work and for rest.

As a "Type A" personality, I always want to be in the mode of *doing.* I even include church as something I want to "do." A dear mentor once reminded me of the story of Jesus teaching the Pharisees that Sunday is not about following rules.

The Sabbath is about refilling the cup.

THE IMPORTANCE OF VACATION

Is a vacation an opportunity to turn into a blob or an opportunity to amplify the daily routines that produce energy?

What I realized is vacation is the opportunity to amplify the activities you struggle to fit in during the typical work day. A good vacation day revolves around life-affirming activities. I try to use vacations as opportunities to improve core areas of my life. For instance, I take that time to be one hundred percent present with my family. I watch very little television and do not allow my phone or the emails it contains to distract me. I put forth the effort to take in all the little moments I am otherwise too busy to appreciate.

I also use vacation time to learn. I drink deeply from books for longer than I usually have the time for, and I create, spending quality time writing in the mornings before everyone wakes up. I have also found this is a great opportunity to reinforce movement in my life, which improves my physical health. Oftentimes, my daily routine puts working out on the back burner.

Finally, vacations are a great chance to secure quality sleep. During this valuable time, I go to bed as early as eight o'clock and wake up fully charged at six o'clock the next morning. This gives me the space to enjoy the morning's stillness. It is a powerful moment in the day and an opportunity to sit with oneself and seek insight.

As Albert Camus tells us in *Create Dangerously*, "Great ideas, it has been said, come into the world as gently as doves…if we listen attentively, we shall hear [them.]"

Vacation time grants us an opportunity to continue to refine the disciplines of a good life. It's not an excuse to let all the good habits disappear. If a vacation is not intentional, it can leave one more tired and maybe even less fulfilled. I'm finding implementing the above core principles leaves me more recharged and also helps me think and dream bigger.

IT'S ALL ABOUT SERVICE

It's important to learn about ourselves and to experience personal growth. When I reach my fullest sense of self, I realize it's not about me. As Victor Frankl put it, "The door to happiness opens outward." It's all about people—*serving* people. It is an act of service. The full circle journey of self-leadership leads us to realize it's not about the person in the mirror; it's about all the people waiting beyond it.

TOUCHING THE SPIRIT

There's a side to leadership we all must take time to acknowledge, and that is the deeper responsibility of touching the spirit of people. "Spirit" does not necessarily mean something religious. Instead, it refers to people's higher selves. It refers to the side of people wanting to make the world a better place.

We have a responsibility as leaders to bring out the music of the underplay. We see the play unfolding in front of us, but there is a beautiful orchestra playing underneath the main stage. May the development of our personal growth lead us to touch the spirits of others. May our ability to touch others give them the courage to believe in greatness.

GROWING CONFIDENCE

I was in the field with an experienced superintendent near the end of my transition as I was about to become president. He asked me, "How are you feeling about taking over at the end of the year?"

For many years, I would have responded with reluctance, uncertainty, and rambling. However, now it was only three months before the official transition. After seven years of intentionally working on myself and investing in my preparation, I embraced a moment of silence to gather my thoughts. "We have such an amazing team," I told him. "Such a great foundation has been set for the future. I'm excited. Yes, of all emotions—excitement is what I'm feeling."

Finding the right balance of hubris and humility has taken many years of intentional development.

CHAPTER SEVEN

"Growth creates complexity and complexity kills growth."
—JAMES ALLEN AND CHRIS ZOOK

The only constant is change. It is the leader's responsibility to work on the business. This is mandatory. No excuses. If no one is working on the business, then irrelevance will spike, and retention will plummet.

THREE DISTINCT HATS

Michael Gerber is the author of *E-Myth*. He opened my framework to the concept of a business owner wearing three distinct hats in a family business: entrepreneur, manager, and technician. Most businesses solely focus on the technician hat. However, working on the business requires picking up the other two hats.

I'm naturally drawn to the entrepreneur hat, but during the succession, I found I was focused on wearing the technician hat. The culture of the business values the technician, so that was the hat I wore to build trust with the team. At the time, my company culture valued the industry expert, not the business builder.

When I first started at Century, I was overwhelmed by the mountain of organizational knowledge I needed to climb. After understanding the distinct roles of technician, manager, and entrepreneur, the burden lifted from my shoulders. I realized I could become a guru of growing the business, and I could foster the growth of the team to carry industry knowledge forward.

The journey of stewardship is about building the team and empowering them to grow the business. The leader does not need to bear the burden of knowing everything and micromanaging the company to succeed. That is not sustainable. It's quite frankly selfish and egotistical to think one person can take on all the various hats required to operate the business and grow the organization for the future.

MAINTENANCE OR MISSIONAL

Status quo or growth?

It's easy to find ourselves in maintenance mode when we've had some success and do not have a clear path to follow. The maintenance mode mindset leaves us hoping to somehow beat the numbers from the year before; we are hoping we are the only bidder.

In other words, the most significant pitfall of maintenance mode is that it leaves us hoping everyone will keep doing what they are doing.

In contrast, missional mode is active. It is intentional. A missional mode mindset promotes discomfort and focuses attention on leading indicators and activities that drive growth.

A missional culture requires a lot of investment in time and seeking counsel from others to create fertile soil for a missional culture.

The paradigm in which a company operates becomes most apparent by the content of its weekly meetings. Is it reporting out what is happening day-to-day? Is it comparing what today looks like to the vision and strategic goals for the quarter, the markers that align with the vision?

BUILDING FOR THE LONG-TERM

"If you want to build for one year from now, grow wheat. If you want to build for ten years from now, grow trees. If you want to build for one hundred years from now, grow people."

—CHINESE PROVERB

Having the clarity required to build for the long haul sets the proper priorities. Growing people grows the company—it's that simple. Working on the business is about building people and cultivating the soil for them to flourish and blossom.

A few good rules of thumb:

1. Hire great people.
2. Cultivate the soil for the team to thrive.
3. Get out of the way.

BEHAVIOR MODIFICATION BUSINESS

Any company without a clear operating system built to systematically work on the business is in the modification business.

"People problems" and lack of clarity create an urgent time suck, draining time and energy away from growing the business.

When you are running a business without a clear mission and without alignment with your people, it stands to reason that finding solutions to those things first can pave the way to a flourishing business down the line.

COMPANIONSHIP VS. LEADERSHIP

Leadership is a skill. Companionship is an instinct. A new manager needs to understand who they are as a person, where the company is going, and the tools required to lead their team.

New managers lean into companionship more than leadership. It's more comfortable to lean into the path of least resistance by blaming "corporate" and doing what's comfortable. Managers do not magically become leaders just by virtue of their title.

BUILDING A COHESIVE TEAM—PERSONALITY, ROADMAP, AND TOOLS

Awareness of Self

Good leaders are mindful of their words and actions. Leadership teams should understand how team members think and communicate to eliminate the potential for things to be misunderstood or taken personally. Everyone is hardwired with their own gifts, world lens, priorities, and communication style. Knowing your team is an essential ingredient to building cohesion.

There are many different paradigms to use for understanding thyself as mentioned earlier:

- DiSC
- Core Value Index
- Enneagram
- Strengths Finders
- Working Genius

All of these frameworks provide language around how an individual digests and perceives the world. There are many other frameworks available. These are the five I have experienced and have enjoyed learning. These paradigms have helped me frame conversations and discussions to help people understand how I am viewing the world or how I am coming to a business decision.

Roadmap

"You're not a team without a purpose."

—HORST SCHULTZ

We can't expect a manager to lead if he doesn't know where he's going. The executive team needs to do the hard work of creating the vision for the rest of the team. We need to give the team the road map before it's needed.

Tools

"We don't rise to the level of our goals. We fall to the level of our training."

—ARCHILOCHUS

There's an old saying, "People get promoted to their level of incompetence."

Yes, they do. That is because leadership is a skill. Again, a person does not transform into a leader when their business card title changes. If a manager is incompetent, it is probably a reflection of the executive leadership team. It is likely they did not provide the manager with the training necessary to move them from companionship to leadership.

An executive leadership team needs to make sure the managers within their company are receiving appropriate training that enables them to step into their role and succeed. Athletes regularly step outside the court and into the weight room to improve their physical capabilities. Similarly, leaders also need to step outside the business and improve their leadership skills.

CLOCK BUILDERS OR TIMEKEEPERS

Jim Collins coined the term *clock builders* when describing those who are building resilient institutions. It is easy to get swept into the current markets and product offerings. The only constant is change, and leadership is required to build each institution for its people rather than defining an institution by a specific product.

Industries and products come and go. Being built to last is being built to change. Clock builders are the ones who create resilient institutions that transcend generations.

Timekeepers are much more likely to have a fixed mindset.

Their vision, even though it may be exciting, is naturally smaller. This is because they have been pigeonholed to a specific product or industry.

Clock builders have an inherent growth mindset because they continue learning from the inevitable failures of business. A clock builder also has a larger vantage point to capitalize on opportunities.

Think of a timekeeper like someone who was breeding horses at the end of the 1800s. Even though automobiles had been invented, they were rare and unreliable. Instead of seeing the writing on the wall, a timekeeper would keep breeding horses—faster, stronger, and more docile.

Everything changed in 1908 when Henry Ford unveiled the Model-T, the world's first affordable automobile. Not only that, when demand skyrocketed, and his employees couldn't fulfill orders, Ford invented the assembly line and eliminated the problem.

Ford was a clock builder. Ford saw an opportunity and began tinkering with the concept of gasoline engines. Later, he met with industry leaders like Thomas Edison and racing experts like Tom Cooper. Finally, when Ford unveiled his most successful invention, it completely changed the world.

I walked into one of our branches two months before my official transition date. As I walked through the facility, I saw the results of much of the hard work I had put in over the years. Prior to that visit, I had only read about them from the reports and programs my teammates used to operate the business.

Every single person in the organization that day was using technology I had implemented in my first five years at the organization. Seeing the vision of digital transformation playing out in real-time—and so successfully—was extraordinarily gratifying.

As president, it has been just as important for me to continue to be a clock builder. I do not want to get pulled into being a timekeeper; I don't want to forget I need to build the clock. It is my role as leader and steward to look ahead of the team.

The worst disservice I can do for the future of the organization is to get sucked into administrative tasks or do what the previous president did because that is "how it was done." We are great, and we're getting better. The act of *delegate to elevate* must always be top of mind to continue to build the clock. My role is to continue to cut down the trees to build the path to make the organization better.

IMPORTANT > URGENT

"My interest is in the future, because I am going to spend the rest of my life there."

—CHARLES KETTERING

During my time in the second chair, it felt like the usual state of operations was constantly putting out fires. We did not have processes or meetings. I had piles of contracts and other papers constantly hitting my desk. Peter Drucker so eloquently stated, "The bottleneck is always at the top of the bottle." The administrative tasks get piled at the top if they are not delegated.

Our family business had been growing over the years, and, like any workplace, it has always been important that everyone "do their job." The only problem was we had not clearly defined everyone's roles. We suffered from the curse of assumptions, believing that people should instinctively know what needs to be done. We expected people to be mind readers, and we were constantly critiquing them rather than coaching them before mistakes could occur.

According to Ashley Goodall and Marcus Buckingham in their bestseller, *Nine Lies About Work*, "We can never create excellent performances by only fixing poor ones. Mistake fixing is just a tool to prevent failure."

We talk about being busy as a good thing, but really, being busy is stupid. When we are constantly in a state of reaction, we are denied the stillness required to create a better business. An executive looking at credit card receipts who chooses to call someone out for a $5 purchase is not seeking work of future value. By reacting instead of processing, that executive isn't seeing what's actually important.

Getting stuck in the urgent also leads to getting stuck in seeking control. in *Nine Lies About Work*, Goodall and Buckingham explain, "Leaders can't be in the control business and must be in the intelligence, meaning, and empowerment business—the outcomes business." Urgent matters put an executive on the production line rather than on the balcony. From the production line, they can't get ahead of the team and build for the future.

Something *important* is equivalent to building future value, while something *urgent* is equivalent to current value. Moving from urgent to important marks a huge shift, one where the focus has shifted from putting out fires to creating a competitive advantage.

Ultimately, I wanted to approach the first chair by seeking the important. That said, I knew my first months as president would require that I handle the urgent. There were metaphorical fires burning everywhere, and I needed to build both systems and employee trust. The company was used to their leader handling urgent matters, so I needed to show competency.

Today, I handle the urgent by training the team around me to problem solve. Ultimately, I hope to be able to empower and train others so they can swiftly handle any urgent issues in my place. For now, however, my involvement is still needed.

Both during the transition and afterward, we need to be able to go from the dirt—the urgent—to the sky—the important. We must not dwell solely in the dirt or refuse to land once we're flying in the sky. We need to be willing to create a transition of culture instead of shoving my preferences front and center.

That said, this kind of flexibility can sometimes be misinterpreted. Unfortunately, ageism is alive and well, though the truth is, age is just a number. The team needs to know I care and that, despite my youth, I am able to handle the ground- and sky-level responsibilities that fall to the first chair leader. This is something I've found I still have to prove even now that I'm president.

In *Switch: How to Change Things When Change Is Hard,* brothers Chip and Dan Heath explain, "A change leader thinks, 'How can I set up a situation that brings out the good in these people?'" This is an excellent question. I want to empower my management team to thrive by answering the urgent rather than creating bureaucracy that has to travel up a flagpole. I want to create a situation of empowerment that will subsequently free up my time. This, in turn, enables me to seek the important, or future value.

It was vital to build my team to handle the urgent with a mastery of the following core framework:

1. What to change: the core problem
2. What to change to: the solution
3. How to cause change: create enthusiasm

Becoming an executive who primarily lives in the space of important matters will take a considerable amount of time. It involves a paradigm shift of how the company operates. In my situation, the previous leadership had built a *hub and spoke model,* which I hoped to uplift over time by empowering the team around me. As Jim Canfield and Kraig Kramers described in *CEO Tools 2.0,* "The pace of the pack can't exceed the pace of the leader." Building in bandwidth for our managers is a critical component of having the ability to spend time in future value.

Fixing an urgent matter is like drinking a milkshake instead of taking the time to eat a wholesome lunch. I always feel horrible thirty minutes later, but the milkshake filled that immediate void. This is a type of quick fix I see in business settings on a daily basis: I see my leadership team grab a milkshake instead of a nutritious lunch.

The attention of a leader is trumped by urgency. The "fires" and the pull to fix moments are ever-present. Saying "yes" to the urgent is saying "no" to the important.

Putting out fires is a wonderful way to validate the self and one's importance in the operations of an organization. A focus on fixing moments creates a hub and spoke model, as mentioned before, regardless of intent. Fixing moments rather than building proper systems buries a leader in the business, thus preventing the leader from actually leading.

Stepping on the balcony to orchestrate systems requires an appreciation for saying "no" to the urgent. Fixing moments is like experiencing a sugar high. It gets the job done in the moment, but you'll regret it later as the systems and people feel the impact of a quick fix and clogs begin to build up.

I stepped into the first chair surrounded by fires. The president who came before me ran on urgency; he loved fires. My presidency marked an incredible culture shift, one we're still working on solidifying and improving today. We are still working to transition from living in urgency to evaluating long-term importance.

It's critical for a leader to be able to see the difference between fixing moments and improving systems. A leader must find time for the important. The screaming, urgent matters may distract the leader from the whispering, important matters that have the power to ultimately improve the business.

As James Clear put it, "We don't rise to the level of our goals. We fall to the level of our systems."

Without proper systems, a business cannot grow or become a resilient organization greater than any one individual.

CHAPTER EIGHT

"Every organization one day will be a software organization as every business and every sector digitally transforms."

—GREG SHAW, JILL NICHOLS, AND
SATYA NADELLA IN *HIT REFRESH*

When I first walked through the doors of Century Fence, the company was still operating off of dot matrix printers, typewriters, emails that had been printed out to be physically shared, and more. We had a long way to go. I remember being given printed documents to review because we could not export any information into Excel from the lackluster accounting systems. The VP of finance would print out emails and walk downstairs from his office to my office, all to deliver a crisp, paper copy of the email.

Wow, we had a lot of work to do in 2015.

Prior to my arrival, mission-critical information was hidden in a filing cabinet or lost in a sea of papers on someone's desk. Duplicative data entry ran rampant. Duplicative spreadsheet files were managed by every department in every location. Nothing was standardized. Nothing was digitized.

Nothing had changed since 1980.

In the first twenty-plus years of the twenty-first century, the process of digitizing and increasing the visibility of data is the big trend of middle market businesses. Most middle market businesses are not investing in "overhead" to streamline operations for the future. In fact, most of them are not building scalable systems for the future. The generation-owning, profitable middle market companies are of the baby boomer generation. They are typically not in tune with the digital revolution and would rather profit and exit the company before investing heavily in technology.

Century Fence is a tech company. No one knows it yet, but we are. We are an information broker. We are putting information at people's fingertips to better serve customers.

SELF-SUFFICIENCY IS POVERTY

"My company is unique…'oh you get paid in Euros.'"

—KARL WILLIAMS

During the seven years I spent in the second chair, I frequently heard comments like "Our business is unique," or "They wouldn't understand." This, while I sought to bring in new ideas, concepts, and resources to the company in an effort to discover new perspectives and insights. For decades before I joined the family business, we lived on a metaphorical island. The average tenure was about twenty years, so fresh ideas were not in the cards.

It was clear that well into the twenty-first century, our company was stuck in the 1980s.

Humility is an essential ingredient to building a resilient company. It is required to change the culture toward learning. Seeing business as a vehicle for constant learning rather than fighting change is a huge shift in culture. Rather than forging ahead with blindfolds on and gritting our teeth, there's a lot to be gained by sitting in stillness and thinking, *how can we improve, and who can we ask for help?*

As leaders, it is essential to appreciate the complexity and the reality of the interconnected nature of the world. The marketplace is always changing and should lead executives to build a culture of seeking counsel and fresh ideas.

There's so much downside to falling into the trap of self-sufficiency. When we are only focused on self-sufficiency, ego becomes infused into the business. It leads to living one year forty times over—this is my biggest nightmare—it is a scary thought. Robin Sharma eloquently frames the issue of learning: "Too many people among us die at 30 and are buried at 80." We only get one life, and failing to enrich it with unique experiences is wasteful. As leaders, we must avoid traveling down comfortable, easy paths that require no learning, development, or even guidance. Self-sufficiency can lead to avoiding growth. Sharma continues, "world-class begins where your comfort zone ends."

Leading a business down a set, well-worn trail occurs most often when you do not actively and intentionally seek new perspectives. It's easy to find comfort in the known. Unfortunately, the trail can become so well-worn that it becomes a trench. When you only do what you know, your blind spots begin to grow significantly.

The landscape of running a business should be a path we know well. That said, leaders should intentionally explore off the path by seeking new information and counsel from others. This creates new, rich experiences and also builds relationships. The self-sufficiency and comfort found in deeply beaten paths leads to poverty in experiences, relationships, and finances, particularly when one's business model becomes irrelevant.

It's imperative to embrace a communal approach of inter-connectedness rather than assume a default posture of individualism. Self-sufficiency leans toward efficiency, but in today's brave new world, adaptation is what is most important.

Doing things *right* is not as important as *doing the right thing*. That is the difference between management and leadership. A desire for and pursuit of self-sufficiency are not compatible with leadership.

Of course, the act of leading and developing people is not simple, nor is it easy.

Dave Olsen, the original Head of Coffee at Starbucks, once famously shared a story describing a National Public Radio journalist seeking to understand the human condition. Howard Behar chronicled Olsen's anecdote in his book, *It's Not About the Coffee*:

> The reporter visited a jet propulsion laboratory and spoke to one of the scientists and posed the question: "What do you people think of when you come up against a problem you can't quite figure out but you think you will or should be able to solve? You can't say it's not rocket science, since you're the

rocket scientist." The scientist responds, "At least it's not brain surgery."

So the reporter paid a visit to the brain surgeons at Johns Hopkins and asked them the same question. After thinking for a hike, the doctors came back with their response, "At least it's not nuclear physics."

So of course the reporter was compelled to talk with the nuclear scientists at some other premier institution. The nuclear physicists were pretty disdainful of the question, but after concentrating on it for a while, they explained that what they say to themselves is, "At least it's not social science."

As we can see, it is a challenge for all leaders of any size organization, and they face this on a daily basis.

SYSTEMS RUN BUSINESS—PEOPLE RUN SYSTEMS

I was recently listening to the popular podcast *How I Built This*, digging into the rise of Curt Richardson's success with Otter-Box. It is now an $8 billion enterprise. It started as a plastic molding business out of Richardson's garage. He struggled for over twenty years to gain traction. Once he gained some momentum, he started struggling even more because, with more people on the team, there were more fires to put out.

As Century Fence continues its momentum of growth, we are facing significant headwinds. Though I have a vision for a better culture, building it is still a challenge. We have fires every day. Prior to my appointment as president, we had no structure during meetings. We only met when there was something urgent to address. Daily fires are not sustainable, especially as my wife and I grow our family unit. I'm also aware that putting out fires is a great way to affirm one's importance and ego. That is not useful. I want to build a business that can sustain itself and allow others to flourish. I want everyone at the company to enjoy a proper work-life balance as well.

After a couple of years of experiencing growth, Richardson came to an inflection point in his career. He decided the day-to-day grind of constantly putting out fires had to change. His paradigm shift and how he approached OtterBox changed his life and allowed OtterBox to have a meteoric rise.

Richardson began a journey of putting systems in place and putting people in the right seats. This created structure, which ultimately led to an environment of clarity. As a result, the business grew and flourished.

Systems are very difficult to put in place. The first step is to define them. While I was sitting in the second chair, I was in my bat cave, putting together the systems I wanted to utilize in the future. I did the deep thinking required, making sure I understood the business. Focusing on the systems and deeply understanding them allowed me to not spend any money—or step on the toes of the president at the time.

Once I stepped into the lead role, I opened up my systems playbook and leveraged my ability to dictate how we invest in people. By understanding people's roles and by having a leadership team focused on systems, we can become people builders. The leadership team does not need to squeeze every ounce of energy out of the employee base, nor must it constantly fix errors. We can get ahead of mistakes and invest in our people to build their skillsets.

THE IMPORTANCE OF SPIRIT

"Better to know who you are than where you are going."

—JIM COLLINS

The core of any business is its spirit. Without a firm grasp of that spirit, it is too easy to get lost in the current of operations and flashy fads. Without the core ideology, a business cannot possibly last, because everything changes so quickly. There must be a constant for a business, and that is its spirit.

Defining values and purpose is not about wordsmithing an inspiring speech or company-wide memo. It is about interpreting what resides deep inside the business. A visionary company is not defined by the products of the day. A visionary company is defined by a deep understanding of its own spirit. These companies identify the mountain they will climb and inspire A-level players to get excited to join the climb.

The mountain may change day-to-day or decade-to-decade, but the direction toward the company's North Star is always understood. It is evergreen. The spirit of the company remains constant—it's everything else that should change!

As Jim Collins once said, "To build an enduring, great company in any era requires being almost obsessive in pursuit of a purpose."

Just months before I was promoted to president, the family

business had the strongest balance sheet it had ever had, but we had not yet articulated the vision or the mountain we were climbing. The lack of clarity felt like we were sailing a ship through a nighttime storm. Burning out is all too real. We grind, and we grind. A lot of A-level players redline throughout the year, and we were teetering on the edge of burnout.

Still, the message was "Push. Push. Push." But for what? We didn't receive clarity regarding what the push was meant to be for. It was just "what we do."

There's a clear line between hard work and workaholism, and when I was in the second chair, it was clear our company did not make that distinction.

My years in the second chair left me pondering how I could fit into the mix. How could I provide value? I certainly wasn't going to tell a foreman how to fix a broken hose on his truck; I wasn't going to micromanage the superintendent on how to correctly fix the hinge on a gate repair job.

What I could do was begin to cultivate an environment in which people could flourish.

We had been blessed with profitability and an opportunity to step beyond those profits, but we were staying in the shallow end of the pool. Though the company enjoyed the experience of being profitable, we had not infused meaning into the organization.

As Jim Canfield and Kraig Kramers put it in *CEO Tools 2.0*, "Profit is simply a strategic necessity rather than the supreme end point." My responsibility as the steward and first chair leader is to institutionalize the spirit of the organization and provide meaning for A-level players to join the vision.

You can make the vision of the company a collaborative discovery, or you can install it from the top down. Both ways can work. Sam Walton and Henry Ford are great examples of a vision cultivated by a single individual. The risk, however, is that this vision is dictated from above and potentially could not get as much buy-in. As far as a collective mission, the United States Constitution is a great example. The risk of this collective approach is that a vision laid out by a committee could lack clarity.

I have taken the path of setting the vision and values of the organization after seven years of intimate listening to all stakeholders in the business: family, employees, customers, and vendors.

CHAPTER NINE

We are 105 years into the business, and we had put in place the vision and values for the company within the first couple of months of my becoming president. The products and services can change over time, but the spirit of the business must remain intact if it is to be a resilient company. People are not robots, and leaders need a foundation on which to make decisions. We don't want to make decisions based on where the wind is blowing on any given day. Rather, we want to make decisions based on principles.

Visionary companies adapt to the marketplace, but their values and priorities remain rock solid. The companies that transcend generations focus their leadership on internalizing the values of the business, and they pass them down from generation to generation. The DNA of an organization must be defined and well-understood by all who operate within it.

John Willard Marriott Sr. not only groomed his son, John Willard Marriott Jr., on the nuts and bolts of his hotel business, he also taught him how to carry on its values. Marriott Sr. actively trained his son on the company's operations but never allowed it to become the sole priority.

True to form, in 1964, Marriott Sr. wrote to employees, "People are #1…" and two decades later, his son wrote the same: "We are in the people business."

Only discussing the nuts and bolts is simply too risky. The company's entire foundation can be lost if its values are not institutionalized and prioritized. It's the soft stuff that makes a company last. The values are the glue.

Johnson & Johnson CEO Jim Burke estimated in the '80s, he spent 40 percent of his time as CEO communicating the values throughout the company. Truly, proper stewardship of an organization's values and vision give guidance and inspiration to the people inside the company.

ADAPTIVE VS. TECHNICAL

There are two types of problems in business, and they are technical problems and adaptive problems. Technical problems are known problems with known solutions. The challenge they present is one of execution. On the other hand, adaptive problems are known issues with unclear solutions. The challenge is to identify them with potential pros and cons. Only afterward can we face the challenge of execution.

My time in the second chair taught me that most of business consists of adaptive challenges at the C-suite level. Adaptive challenges require a cohesive team to honestly find solutions in the fog of human institutions.

Business is messy. Naming the type of problem is critical because it establishes some order within the chaos. Businesses often take the approach of assuming every problem is a nail. To that end, they tend to attempt to solve each problem the same way: with a hammer. Unfortunately, most problems require access to an array of tools.

DEVELOPING TALENT

A company is a team. It's a group of people working together toward a common goal or mission. Most companies are buried in the urgent and never take the time to work on their people.

It seems like a simple and intuitive concept to have clear goals, a vision, a mission, and so on. What I've come to appreciate in the family and middle market space of businesses is that this is very rare. Most small- to medium-sized businesses are buried in the day-to-day grind. Every problem and task is treated as its own unique situation rather than elevating to a higher level of attitude to see the business as a set of processes.

A manager at my family business recently retired after dedicating forty years to the company. He shared with me, "The business is the easy part, and the people are the hard part." With this reality, we need to do something about it and allocate leadership efforts accordingly!

That said, in the search for and cultivation of talent, sometimes we discover people who aren't a good fit. The act of firing toxic attitudes is the Archimedes Lever of changing culture. People with poor attitudes are like holes in a helium balloon—they drain the energy and excitement from the business.

In a family business, there are people who have been "untouchable." Oftentimes, they are good performers with bad attitudes. It takes guts to let these types of people go with grace.

I believe a three-pronged approach should be taken:

- Build a compensation system.
  - Payouts should be frequent and above market so employees see they are taken care of and receive payment punctually in accordance with performance.
- Create a recognition system.
  - Recognize people five times more than they are criticized.
- Provide training and tools.
  - Shower employees with training and tools so they may better serve the customer.

All three of these strategies exist outside the norm of a typical business because deploying them requires strategy, intentionality, and bandwidth.

THROUGHPUT > COST CUTTING

The mainstream business sentiment focuses on the belief that "overhead is a killer." I think this framework leads to a lack of critical thinking and a cursory view of expenditures that seeks to minimize for the sake of "cutting costs."

If we consider a business like a link of chains, each department represents a distinct and dependent chain in the sales cycle. The average manager will simply weigh the chains and seek to cut the weight. A savvy manager will seek to understand the strength of the links. That manager will make sure to reinforce the weak points and increase weight at the strongest connections.

It's easy to hyper-focus on operational expenses. Cash outflow is a tangible measurement we can use to squeeze and seek to optimize.

A common focus of OPS:

1. Operational expense (money out the door)
2. Inventory (money stuck in the system)
3. Throughput (incoming money)

A better way to focus a company is to flip the priorities around:

1. Throughput
2. Inventory
3. Operational expense

Flipping the focus forces all who are involved in making decisions to see the system as a whole and to maximize cash inflow. Strategic decisions can be made on the balcony. We don't have to put managers under the microscope to make decisions at a local level with no sense of unintended consequences on the larger goal of maximizing throughput.

- Throughput
- Inventory
- Operational

Growing up as an athlete, I constantly heard the following from my coaches: "We are as good as our weakest link." It's quite the cliche, yet it absolutely rings true in the universe of capitalism.

Every department within a company in the process of converting a customer order into cash is a crucial link in the process. If any department experiences a bottleneck, then the company is only as good as that struggling department.

Below is a common manufacturing-dependent process:

1. Sales
2. Purchasing
3. Superintendent
4. Shop: Manufacturing/Assembly
5. Shipment
6. Installation

Every step and department presents an opportunity for a screw-up. Wherever the bottleneck occurs in the sales cycle, that place should be evaluated and provided additional resources. These additional resources should be allocated, or the process creating the bottleneck should be reconsidered.

When making decisions as a manager, the focus should be on the connections between the dependent events or departments. The focus should be on the connections between the chains rather than on the weight of the chain as a whole.

EMBRACING "AND"

Business is messy and full of competing forces or polarities. Balance is not necessarily the right answer for all situations.

The institutions that can lean into the conflicts listed below will thrive in the twenty-first century. The global and digital economy of today is not a scarce world full of "or" but rather, an abundant economy full of "AND."

Howard Schultz set a great example when he returned to the leadership scene at Starbucks. What struck me as the most profound aspect of his story—and turnaround of the business—was his acknowledgment of the polarities surrounding his turnaround. The greatest visionary companies do not balance competing interests with an "or" mentality. Instead, they seek to thrive and lean into both sides of the competing forces.

Schultz leaned into the polarities. These are the ones he so eloquently shared in his book *Onward*:

- Shareholder value AND social conscience
- Profit AND humanity
- Local AND global
- Innovation AND heritage
- Tradition AND modern-day relevance
- Cut costs AND invest
- Efficiency AND romance
- Head held high AND feet firmly planted
- Encouraging AND pushing
- Entrepreneur vision AND patient execution
- Entrepreneur enthusiasm AND rigor complex organizations

To build on this, Jim Collins articulated the forces visionary companies are able to lean into in his book, *Built to Last*:

- Change AND stability
- Conservative AND bold
- Low cost AND high quality
- Creative autonomy AND consistency
- Invest in future AND do well in short-term
- Purpose beyond profit AND pragmatic pursuit of profit
- Fixed core ideology AND vigorous change AND movement
- Conservatism around the core AND bold, committing, risky moves
- Clear vision AND sense of direction AND opportunistic experimentation
- Big Hairy Audacious Goals AND incremental evolutionary progress
- Selection of managers steeped in the core AND selection of managers that induce change
- Ideological control AND operational autonomy
- Extremely tight culture AND ability to change, move, AND adapt
- Investments for the long term AND demands for short-term performance
- Philosophical, visionary, futuristic AND superb daily execution of "nuts AND bolts"
- Organization aligned with a core ideology AND organization adapted to its environment

INSTITUTION-BUILDING

Organizing humans to accomplish a mission is the recipe of all meaningful accomplishments in history.

In the business world, we get caught up in the game of capitalism and do not prioritize developing the skills necessary to build a cohesive and enthusiastic team.

Nothing can be done without the people.

Human flourishing in business requires an intentional leader who seeks to care for the whole employee as a person. Checking the box of compensation is the first level. Providing an environment for a person to do meaningful work and be appreciated is the second essential box. All of us have an unquenchable thirst to feel a sense of belonging—it is instinctual and tribal.

Institution building at its essence is tribe-building. Whether you're in the first or second chair at your company, ask yourself, *how am I building my tribe?*

INNOVATION AND CHANGE

It is intimidating to think about how to initiate innovation. Look at Amazon, Google, Sony, 3M, and all the multi-billion dollar organizations.

It's helpful to think of innovation through the lens of evolution. In *On the Origin of Species*, Charles Darwin wrote, "To my imagination, it is far more satisfactory to look at [well-adapted species] not as specially endowed or created instincts, but as small consequences of one general law leading to the advancement of all organic beings—namely, multiply, vary, let the strongest live and the weakest die."

Darwin's findings in the 1800s are freeing. A leader does not need a masterful and perfect plan. Simply seek purposeful, forward momentum by putting mechanisms into place that encourage forward motion and unabashed curiosity.

The real world is ambiguous, foggy, and muddy. None of us likes to stumble, but stumbling can only happen if we—or our company—are moving forward. Maintaining the right posture is more important than a grand, sterile plan written by a consulting firm.

I find the day-to-day requirements of running a business extraordinarily hectic. Theory can only go so far. Theory and a strategic plan only work to a certain extent. Building tangible mechanisms into the DNA of the organization is a more effective way to push forward, incremental motion.

Evolution is true innovation. Incremental and spontaneous is the reality. We must be willing to experiment and tweak our experiments, as Henry Ford did when developing the Model-T. There is no grand plan. The answers are in the mud. High-level direction can come from the sky, but the answers are scattered on the ground and need to be fostered to bear fruit.

The 3M company instituted many different mechanisms to ensure innovation. Phrases the company has published reinforce this ideology:

- "If you put fences around people, you get sheep. Give people the room they need."
- "Encourage; don't nitpick. Let people run with an idea."
- "Hire good people, and leave them alone."

Visionary companies harness the power of evolution by fertilizing the soil that unlocks human initiative. They appreciate that the products or services that got them here may not get them *there*, to the next goal or place of success.

Here are some examples of company **evolutions:**

- **3M:** mining → sticky notes and adhesives
- **Marriott:** soda → hotels and hospitality
- **J&J:** medical products → consumer products
- **HP:** electronic measurement equipment → computers
- **IBM:** measuring scales → computers
- **Boeing:** military aircrafts → commercial aircrafts
- **American Express:** freight → financial services
- **Motorola:** battery eliminators → mobile phones
- **Disney:** animation → amusement parks, toys, and clothing

These massive company transitions were undoubtedly difficult at first. Simply put, change is loss. It is a loss of security, a loss of what is comfortable and familiar.

The media and tech companies make it appear as though change is something that can be accomplished quickly. Directives like *fail fast*, *ask forgiveness*, and *break it and we'll fix it* don't reflect reality.

Why? Because change is loaded with emotion. Change requires the utmost compassion. If change is not facilitated with nuance and care, then the culture and the leader can lose a lot of credibility.

Change has a three-step arch:

1. Loss: show compassion
2. Transition: collaborate for the future
3. New beginning: establish best-in-class processes

In order to help people get to the end goal of a new beginning, leaders need to provide security and help people feel heard. This is especially true for those who are experiencing feelings of loss as a result of change. Then, the leader can get the team involved in helping build a brighter future. Making the journey collaborative can enhance feelings of security, pride, and ownership of big changes. In this way, change can become a signal of growth instead of a signal of threat.

THE POWER OF HUMBLE INQUIRY

The quality of a question leads to the quality of the conversation. Great questions lead to great answers.

A leader needs to spend more time asking questions than issuing orders.

To that end, the act of *humble inquiry* leads to a better understanding of situations and positioning.

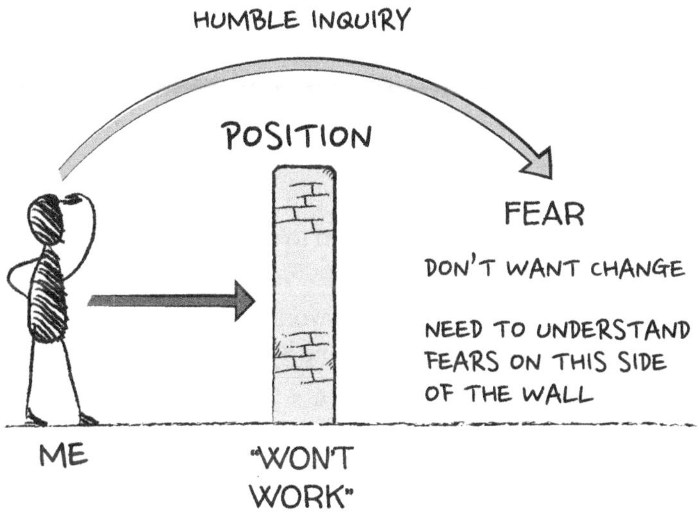

COMMAND AND CONTROL CULTURE

When you treat people like children, they will act like children. Businesses stuck in a paternalistic worldview where "the owner knows best" are archaic. Some companies dictate everything from the amount invested into retirement accounts to time off and more without any room for negotiation. This kind of restrictive micromanagement leads to unhappy employees who—rightfully so—cannot understand why they shouldn't be trusted to make their own choices.

The command and control leadership style is eroding. The workforce of the twenty-first century is requiring a voice in the organization. The organizations to adapt quickest will win the war for talent. A forward-thinking company's soil needs to be fertilized for A-level players who are willing to work and think as autonomous, intelligent adults.

Acknowledging paternalistic culture is the first step toward changing it. I appreciate the care the previous generations provided to our employees. I also realize we need to continue to evolve the way we interact with our employees and continue to build upon the trust we provide employees.

As today's leaders, we must begin to question all our assumptions and continue the practice for years to come. As Ricardo Semler said in *Maverick*, "Fixed working hours, organization charts, and policy manuals are all so negative. They strip away freedom and give nothing in return but a false feeling of discipline and belonging. They elevate bureaucrats and ennoble conformity. By all means establish and promote a common goal, but recognize divergence and let people determine their own ways of achieving it."

Shifting a culture from paternalistic to collaborative requires a level of trust not often found in business. It is a difficult concept to execute but an exciting journey. It's a journey of moving from a transactional to a transformational environment.

FUTURE OPERATING SYSTEM

Any discussion of changing or working on the business must be prefaced with my utmost gratitude for those who have come before. My thoughts and desire to improve the business would not be possible without the grind and countless hours of the team. My introduction of a future framework comes from a soft heart seeking to make the company more resilient in the ever-changing world. I hope to build a framework bigger than any one person, with a system adaptable to the marketplace and the needs of the team and community.

Prior to my presidency, the company operated under a model built for one person to have all the information. It was a model built around one leader rather than a system built to serve a mission. The world has changed, and today, that system—no matter how successful it was before—will stifle the growth of the company in the years to come.

Legacy Model (i.e., Hub and Spoke Model)

The hub and spoke model has its pros and cons. One of the few positive aspects of this framework is it allows one leader to have complete control. I can imagine a founder of a business naturally growing with this paradigm to make sure the business services customers in the infancy stages and is able to meet payroll at the end of the week.

As Century Fence continues to grow, I have seen the bottleneck that this model unintentionally creates. The growth of the company would be stifled with this model in the years to come because my bandwidth would be a constraint of the increased volume and complexity of the business. This model also creates a very political environment focused on the wishes and needs of the leader rather than the mission and best interests of the company. Living in this model is difficult because all roads lead to one person. All conversations lead to one person making a decision. Jim Collins calls this model the "one genius and a thousand helpers." It may not be the intent, but it becomes the reality when there is no autonomy or empowerment for others.

The future model will be built around the basics of Gino Wickman's Entrepreneurial Operating System (EOS). Every great company has an intentional operating system with a clear purpose of coordinating and driving through the company:

- Meetings
- Goals
- Accountability
- Metrics
- Alignment
- Collaboration

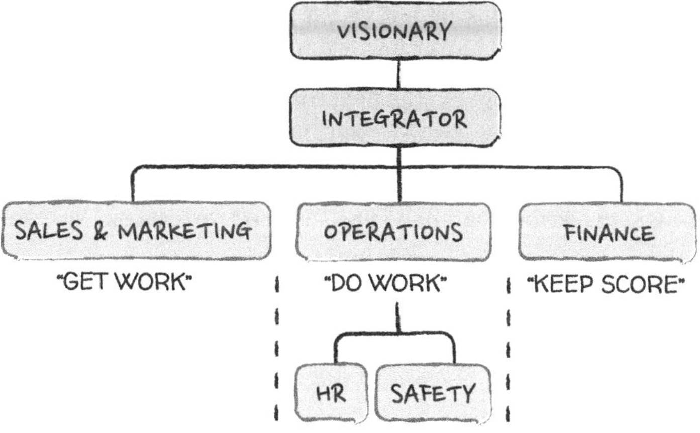

Empowerment comes through clarity and autonomy. We have begun the journey of building out our vision and values so the organization can lean into a new operating system to achieve the vision.

Employees who are empowered to take risks and make the right decisions:

- Ask permission at thresholds:
  - X spending levels
  - Y decision authority levels
- Trust they can make mistakes and can ask for and receive forgiveness

The changing of the framework is appreciated by the team because the past doesn't equal the future. Further, it's important to understand that good times mask poor performance. As a company, we have done a heck of a job capitalizing on the good times. However, developing a strong future operating system will open up opportunities to increase revenue streams and new profitability. This is very important because, now that I'm out of the second chair and firmly seated in the first, this is where we are going in the next three to five years. We will be building systems to delegate and elevate. Every teammate will be positioned at their highest and best use while empowering others to take on new challenges to keep everyone on the team engaged and excited for a bright future.

PART THREE

IN BUSINESS

CHAPTER TEN

Executives have far too many tactical and administrative items on their schedule...adrenaline addiction, the need to stay occupied with moment to moment activities."

—PATRICK LENCIONI

Leading into and in the first period of my presidency the day-to-day operations can best be described as consequential. The result of not having an explicit operating system with an explicit rhythm of meetings causes most of the day to be a function of jumping from issue to issue. The day-to-day feels and might even look like the executives are "adrenaline junkies." The urgent moments always supersede the important, strategic moments. Executives are jumping from one issue to the next, leaving very little opportunity for stillness and improvement initiatives of the operations.

In the beginning of my presidency, we were constantly stuck in the process of putting out fires. Every day presented a new and "exciting" fire. Decisions always bubbled to the top of the organization. It may have created a sense of importance, but it also created issues. For a long time, I couldn't sit in my office for more than ten minutes without getting a phone call to fix something or help make a decision.

A dear mentor of mine helped me appreciate these two distinct systems:

1. Consequential: starter system
2. Intentional: next level system

My company was stuck in the starter system classification, focused on the tasks at hand and making sure we got the bid to the customer before the due date; making sure we processed payroll before the end of the week; making sure materials had arrived for the projects on the schedule; making sure we billed our customers and chased down the money; making sure we had enough money in the bank to pay our vendors.

We were in a constant state of trying to meet deadlines. Fortunately, the economy has been good to the construction business during my tenure, and we've been able to experience growth by being in the right place at the right time.

Getting buried in the details of the starter system is truly exhausting. In my situation, I believe the lemon had been squeezed as hard as it could be squeezed. The system needed to change eventually, and this will be my mark in the years to come as we transition to an intentional operating system. We will plant trees before we need the shade instead of running to find a tree when we realize we need to get out of the sun.

During my time of succession, I found myself leaning into the starter system. Though it didn't represent what I wanted in the long term, it was important to be okay with fixing the moments rather than solving the systemic problems. Becoming a masterful tactician has been my goal to live and thrive within the legacy system before having my turn to evolve the culture and implement an operating system. Leaning into the existing processes has been an opportunity to learn from the legacy leadership of my grandfather and the president who came before me while also building trust and relationships with the entire company for the years to come.

BUSINESS 101—SIMPLE

I think business is really quite simple and often gets over-complicated when we are finding ways to add value to the company. During my seven years of working in the business, I have found a simple framework no one ever taught me in school:

1. Get work: sales and marketing
2. Do work: operations and logistics
3. Keep score: accounting and administrative

Simple mental models are a great tool. Keeping business simple leads to better execution. Simplicity is genius.

LEAN FORWARD AND DANCE

The only way is forward. It is not possible to be a pessimistic CEO and still be met with success. A leader must represent optimism and resilience, and as leaders, there is no other option. Doubt and fear are never nonexistent. How we respond to the fear and the doubt defines leadership in the business.

The difference between a coward and a hero is the willingness to dance with fear. Good leaders lean forward. Even better, the act of leaning forward is infectious. Optimism can be easily shared and is capable of spreading throughout an organization.

ROCKEFELLER'S SILENCE

John D. Rockefeller was known for his discipline. Specifically, he was able to keep his mouth shut and listened more than he spoke. Rockefeller was a master of his emotions, words, and body language. Silence is a powerful tool in business. Active listening is a critical aspect of leading within an organization because teammates must be heard. Directives from the ivory tower are not a productive leadership model.

During my time in the second chair, it was a great time to be an active listener and develop a deeper understanding of where the company should go in the future. Listening and being disciplined in my ability to honor the current regime while I was not in charge was a reflection of my leadership. The ability to follow is also a skill of a leader. On a daily basis, I sought to take the Rockefeller approach and realize I would be able to bend the culture and make necessary changes in the future.

Silence is strength. As I gain maturity, I am much more skilled at restraining my initial thoughts. A leader must be able to abstain. Mastering the discipline of silence is a valuable tool.

After all, silence is found in a leader who is secure.

CARRY THE BAGS

As I've already mentioned, when I was a senior in college, founder Bob Jepson visited my class for a Q&A session. In addition to my prior question, I asked him, "What advice do you have for a college senior entering the workforce?"

Jepson replied with an invaluable piece of advice: "Carry the bags."

Carrying the bags is the act of building trust and relational equity. Carrying the bags signals a willingness to get one's hands dirty and gives an aspiring leader a better understanding of the business and the people within the business. Further, it grants a superpower: empathy. With this, leaders are empowered to make effective decisions for the most important asset in a business: its people.

Carrying the bags is the first step toward becoming a leader people can trust.

A leader builds trust through competence and benevolence. The act of carrying the bags reflects the competence to do the necessary things to serve the company while also having the humility and kindness to chip in to get the company from here to there.

MARKETING 101

I took some business classes in college, but none of the classes stressed the importance of marketing. Marketing brings awareness to a brand or company. Marketing is the first step in the lifecycle of a sales cycle. Without awareness, there is no sale. Without sales, there is no business.

In the twenty-first century, we are bombarded with ads and notifications, so we short circuit when confronted with them. The most effective way for a company to interrupt a prospect from staying on the path of least resistance and entice them to take a risk on a new brand or company is through tension.

Tension creates the initiation for pattern interruption. Without tension, people will remain on the common, well-known path. A good marketer:

- is able to create tension;
- helps tell the story of a bargain; and
- helps a prospect articulate what they want to reach a desired emotion.

IT'S THAT SIMPLE, IT'S THAT HARD

Business is about how people feel...it's that simple and that hard.

We focus so much of our effort on technical smarts. The best leaders and best businesses crack the code of building a culture that affirms their employees and underscores their immense value and importance.

A leader focused on empathy and stewardship strives to cultivate an ever-present sense of belonging and value for every member of the team. Roses do not grow in a happenstance environment, but weeds certainly can. For this reason, leaders must infuse their words and actions with intent and affirmation.

Taking care of employees leads to employees taking care of the customers.

How are you building and investing in your team?

HIRE SLOW, FIRE FAST

The first step to forming a great company is ensuring you've got the right people in the right seats.

Bad apples bring down the whole team. The biggest issue with keeping a bad apple on the team is it communicates to the "A" players that bad behavior is tolerated. If bad behavior is tolerated, then bad behavior is the standard. "A" players will find a company where the standards are properly upheld.

We are learning to hold people accountable even if it is temporarily uncomfortable because the long-term upside is uplifting to the culture. Standards are defined by what leaders tolerate.

The company leader needs to be constantly evaluating the players on their team. The leader is in charge of growing the people, and the business can only grow as the capacity of its people grows.

A solid executive knows when to develop or replace. Here are some questions Jim Collins provides in his book, *BE 2.0*:

1. Are you beginning to lose other people by keeping this person?
2. Do you have a values, will, or skills problem?

3. What's this person's relationships with mirror (taking ownership) and window (blaming others)?
4. Does this person see work as a job or responsibility?
5. Has confidence gone up or down this year?
6. Do you have a bus (person not a good fit) problem or a seat (wrong role) problem?
7. How would you feel if the person quit?

My company is becoming better at the uncomfortable conversations so we can push against status quo. We have begun to document processes and open up the silos of knowledge hidden throughout the organization. Transparency is allowing managers to hold the right people accountable and makes it more feasible to let people go if needed.

With transparency, nobody's lost in the dark.

We are starting to be very particular and intentional with our hires. We are not seeking people out of desperation to fill a role. Instead, we are seeking and recruiting people who want to grow.

BUILDING GOODWILL

What does building goodwill look like? It looks like breaking bread, sending a note, or asking a question about a teammate's child. It's a manager encouraging teammates to take an early Friday afternoon departure to spend time with family and giving people a day off to take care of a sick family member without keeping score.

People are incredible, and investing goodwill with them is one of the best moves you can make. Giving people flexibility and connection builds loyalty and enhances productivity.

Connecting at such an inherent, human level seems basic but is profound. Imagine a team willing to run through a brick wall for your company. Imagine how valuable and impactful that could be. In my first couple of days as president, I had a teammate text me: "where's the brick wall?"

It's never a bad time to take a moment to reflect on what you are doing to build goodwill with your team. There are a few things I've discovered that make these connections even stronger.

THE POWER OF NAMES

One of my main points of focus is to make sure I know everyone's name. If we're at an event, I endeavor to address everyone by their name. It makes a huge difference. Taking the time to learn and use people's names helps them feel a huge sense of belonging.

Nobody likes to feel like they are just a number in the system. Remembering someone's name alleviates this and builds an immense amount of trust. Going to company events, I have started the practice of having an attendee list with all the names of employees, spouses, and kids if they are in attendance.

LOOK IN THE MIRROR WHEN THINGS GO WRONG

One of the most important things a leader can do is take ownership of their mistakes. This isn't always easy, but its effect is significant.

A few years ago, I failed to properly approve payroll for a group of employees. Understandably, many people called in the following Monday asking where their money was and what they should do about their overdraft charges.

As a human being, my heart crashed into my stomach. As a leader, I was very upset and embarrassed. Obviously, it's imperative to ensure the team is paid for a myriad of reasons, and this failure was entirely my own. Accordingly, I took ownership and used it as an opportunity to connect with the employees I inconvenienced. I called every single team member and told them I messed up. This one was on me, and I needed them to know I took their talent, time, and paychecks seriously, and I thanked each employee for their understanding.

Looking in the mirror and taking ownership turned a bad situation into an opportunity to practice humility and connection. It became an opportunity to improve the relational equity and company brand rather than dismissing the incident as "another thing corporate did wrong."

The mistake could have been brushed under the rug. I could have "protected" myself by allowing the blame to become a general mark against the company. Instead, I owned it and addressed it with each employee to let them know I care. The mistake was an opportunity to connect at a personal level with each teammate I affected. The mistake served as an opportunity for me to call teammates individually to show my humility and my willingness to learn from my mistakes. It was a moment of seeking grace from my team and showing the team I care about them and will not brush mistakes to the side. I was willing to look in the mirror and own it.

CHAPTER ELEVEN

The average age of the employees we hire is plummeting. When I first started working at Century, I was the second youngest employee working at our headquarters. Everyone else in the building had been working there for over a decade, except for one other recent college graduate on the team.

Not long ago, we hired two freshly minted graduates, and I spent half the day with each of them. I was amazed at how much the systems and processes have changed over the past five or so years. Every system at Century Fence is digital, and we have so many powerful tools for the future. These graduates didn't even question the programs we were using. The systems are a "no-brainer" because they are efficient and digital.

It has been an emotionally exhausting labor of love to update Century Fence to a digital, Gen-Z-friendly work environment. It takes these young professionals a very short time to become fluent in new systems. They adapt quickly and usually require very little training. Therefore, our biggest challenge is keeping them engaged and feeling appreciated. This is very doable but requires that the leadership team stays ahead of the business, building future value. We must forge a path and illuminate enough of the way forward to attract and inspire these talented, A-level players.

The biggest job killer is anonymity. We need to foster the youth movement by constantly cheering on our young employees, reminding them they are an important part of Century's success.

FLYING AT THE RIGHT ALTITUDE

It is not about being hands-on and hands-off. It's not a binary decision to either be in the mud or be in the sky. We must remain flexible and strike a balance of the proper altitude.

Striking this balance proved challenging during my leadership transition. My predecessor was a very hands-on, nuts and bolts kind of guy. Anything outside this framework was seen as hands-off. In seeking the best way to find balance, I discovered *The Art of the Start 2.0* by Guy Kawasaki and found it very helpful.

Kawasaki described three different elements to make his point: the US military's B1-B Lancer, the Navy SEALs, and the A-10 Warthog.

The B1-B Lancer is a long-range bomber for intercontinental missions, capable of penetrating sophisticated defense systems. It can fly up to thirty thousand feet above the ground and costs $200 million to produce. Navy SEALs are people who specialize in on-the-ground, special operations in enemy territory. Finally, the A-10 Warthog is a plane designed to provide close air support for troops. This simple, rugged machine hits a sweet spot when flying at a thousand feet and costs $13 million to produce.

Of these three examples, leaders should strive to be the A-10 Warthog. It is vital that we exercise our ability to help support our team while maintaining enough of an aerial view to see the future. We want to provide leadership but not manage and own every element of the process—there are SEALs and Lancers for that; there are specialized people for that. Seeking to be an A-10 Warthog requires the confidence to empower others, the competence to understand what is going on, and the curiosity to ask the right questions.

There are a few questions we can ask our teams in order to pinpoint where supportive leadership might be needed:

- Any surprises so far?
- Where are you feeling the least confident?
- Do you have the tools at your disposal to succeed?

We don't want to stay in the weeds, but we do want to be able to dig in when we are needed. The ability to swoop in and provide targeted support can make a meaningful difference.

JOIN THEM ON THE FRONT LINES

"The world belongs to the few people who are not afraid to get their hands dirty."

—ELENA AGUILAR

I was not given any instructions when I first started in the family business. I was thrown at the front lines, working with crews in the field. I was in the heat of battle with the individuals who get things done. My focus as the "owner's grandson" had been to be present in order to best serve. At the time, I did not know anything about the business or its people. I simply jumped into the mud and sought to exemplify hard work.

Getting my hands dirty proved to be the best way to build relational equity with the team. If I hadn't had my finger on the pulse of the people operating on our front lines, things would have decayed. I fully appreciated the work of getting up at 3:30 a.m. and working until 8:00 p.m., only to wake up again the next day and do it all again. There was never a day in the field that I thought was a waste of time. No matter what, I built relational equity that will last for years to come.

Even today, I still carve out time to go to the field. I never want to forget how essential it is. As leaders, we never want to lock ourselves in an ivory tower, setting strategy and issuing memos without a clue of what's really happening.

Every time we join our team on the front lines, we're depositing relational equity into a metaphorical bank account. The time invested by working in the mud allows me to lead from a place of collaboration rather than leading from a place of status or power—things that could wither and collapse over time. The willingness to get my hands dirty shows humility and increases my empathy for the amazing work of the team.

All work is honorable work. All work has dignity. As George Horace Lorimer wrote in *Letters from a Self-Made Merchant to His Son*, "The only undignified job I know of is loafing."

Bestselling author Tim Keller explained the same concept from another angle in *Every Good Endeavor*: "All work has dignity because it reflects God's image in us." In fact, the theologian went on to say, "[Leaders]...should place a high value on all human work, done by all people as a channel of God's love for His world."

Getting in the mud and doing the lifting with your frontline team is the best way to accumulate the experience necessary to go back to the boardroom and establish vision and strategy. It's not possible to know what to do in the boardroom when the front line is an unknown entity.

At the heart of servant leadership, there is a deep appreciation for all aspects of an operation. A lot of companies figure the mud is the area of the business that can figure itself out. Yet, that is precisely where the magic happens. The efforts of the people laboring on the front lines are what drive the customer experience.

Canfield and Kramers's *CEO 2.0* offers some great ideas on how to tap into the brilliance of an organization by engaging with team members on the front lines. He refers to it as walk the four corners—W4C

W4C Questions:

- What do you see that I may not see?
- How can we make things better for customers?
- How can we improve productivity in this area?
- How can we grow faster?

I have never regretted time spent in the field with the team. They make magic happen on the front lines.

Even as I was approaching the transition date of officially becoming president, I intentionally scheduled time to be in the field with the superintendents and other field personnel. The last months of my second chair journey were spent making people feel heard and showing them that I care about them—because I genuinely do. I always want the team to feel my energy and my passion for people. I want people to feel inspired, safe, and fulfilled at the end of a hard day of work.

Walk the four corners. It's time well invested. Always.

BE KIND

To be kind is to be useful. To be useful implies understanding others, understanding what is needed. This implies humble listening.

As a leader, it's so easy to justify kindness in a vacuum. But at its core, kindness is understanding what is needed to be most useful to the team.

Kindness is not softness. It is a deep appreciation for context and the needs of the greater mission at hand. This brings me to an important point:

Be *human*.

We are all human beings. If you treat humans like humans, they respond like humans.

It's so easy to get caught up in the numbers. As companies work to get people to operate at their best, it might be wise to take a moment to remember the human element of it all. Success might just be as simple as treating people like human beings.

DREAMS

Currently, the labor shortage is the worst it has ever been. Every radio ad and billboard is a company seeking workers. Employers, including Century Fence, are providing sign-on bonuses just to have people show up to work. The world is changing in a dramatic, daily fashion, and it can be next to impossible to find people to fill roles. The companies that can connect work with fulfilling personal dreams will win the war for securing talent.

People need the following from their employer:

- Meaningful work
- A feeling of progress
- The belief they're moving toward fulfillment

Dreams are at the core of every person, and they are the currency of the future. By facilitating personal dreams, we push people forward. In turn, these very same people become empowered and energized to push the organization forward. Those who can connect dreams to the day-to-day grind of work will win in the years to come.

Sometimes, that means looking at things differently. It has been my goal, for instance, to build a culture of openness, one that does not automatically shut down ideas that might "cost money."

I want *everyone* to bring ideas to the table. I want everyone to feel they have an opportunity to grow personally and professionally within the company.

I have not constructed the formula for connecting dreams to the day-to-day grind, but it is a part of my journey in the years to come to make this a reality for the team. Everyone deserves a work environment where they can be and become the best version of themselves.

PAYROLL IS THE INVESTMENT PORTFOLIO

What if we paid *above* the market average because we expect above average market performance? Then, what if we treated people so well that they didn't look for other work and didn't want to leave?

The biggest investment in a company is payroll. Payroll is typically viewed as a cost, while at the same time, companies state their people are their biggest asset. I believe payroll is even more important than that. People need to be invested in to feel inspired and be able to go home at the end of the day fulfilled.

Leaders have a tremendous opportunity to help transform our communities by helping teammates feel empowered. They can invest in the special people on their team to help them grow to be able to grow the business.

The most dangerous approach and probably the most common

is: "What is the least amount of money I can pay this person?" When people are treated as a commodity, it is a wasted opportunity to transform that person and the people they touch in their respective family and within the community.

We are in a war for talent, and most people are looking for companies that treat them like human beings and not commodities.

The focus of payroll as an overhead account comes from the obsession with a cost-focused management style. Most managers focus on expenses in isolation. The proper alignment of priorities should take into account the interdependent paradigm discussed in Chapter Nine:

1. Throughput (money coming in)
2. Inventory (money stuck inside system)
3. Operational expenses (money that must be paid)

We focus solely on the costs because this is what we physically see every week when we write checks to vendors, employees, and so on. By switching the mindset to focusing on growing and looking at increasing throughput, we begin to see opportunity in our people rather than the cost of cash going out the door.

Seeing opportunity in employees allows for growth.

I lead a capital intensive construction company. We spend a lot of money on maintaining iron but have, historically, invested very little on the people who run the equipment.

Now that we know this, Century Fence is transforming. We are going to be investing in our people as intentionally as we have been investing in the iron for the trucks.

People are precious and ultimately take their work experiences home to their families. For a company to flourish, the people inside the business must flourish. That's the job of the leader to cultivate the soil for this to be a reality.

WHO ARE WE KEEPING HAPPY?

The hub and spoke model leads to politics. If all decisions in a company are prefaced with, "Will this make the president happy?" you'll hit a dead end. That's an unhelpful, anxious thought process.

I don't want people to think, "Will this make Matt happy?" I want people to think first, "Is this best for Century?" and then, "Will this make *me* happy?" I want my workers to be happy with their contribution for the sake of *their* goals and fulfillment, not mine.

It's not about me. It has taken some time to begin reprogramming the thought process of the team to make it about the company and not about the president, but it has been worthwhile.

When I moved out of the second chair and into the first, our leadership model changed accordingly. I wanted our focus to be on meeting our team's needs and empowering them to care about the company where they spent so much time. At first glance, one might think it is an easy transition to let people voice their opinions and make decisions. However, I learned it isn't as easy as flipping a switch. Paradoxically, though I want people to focus on the team, many of the employees continue framing their decisions toward "What will make Matt happy?" and "What does Matt want to hear?"

But what would make me happy is if they stopped focusing on what would make me happy!

It will take a lot of time and patience to allow people to adjust their thought processes. I understand change is alarming, even when it's a good thing. People in leadership positions also need to experience a sense of psychological safety as they transition to a space of candid collaboration.

Giving people the opportunity to unleash their gifts requires psychological safety and trust. This could take a year. It could take even longer, but Century Fence is determined to give people the time they need to flourish.

MASTER SHOP TALK

The vernacular of day-to-day operations cannot be undervalued. Shop talk is the language of the team. Understanding the language of your team helps people to know you understand. If you understand, then people feel heard, and trust is fostered.

I had to work to learn and embrace shop talk. I still can get a lot better, but I've learned our shop talk includes:

- Product references
- Truck numbers
- Nicknames for employees

- Express pulse on the workload and how it is felt by employees
- Referring to customers with the terms employees in OPS appreciate
- Understanding the projects and schedules the teams are on each week
- Current "problem" jobs

Your mileage may vary, as every industry and every company develops something of their own language. Regardless, mirroring shop talk is an important way to connect with the team. It's an understated skill and an important language to develop fluency in. It must be taken seriously if we are to be taken seriously as leaders.

TEACHING BUFFALO TO FLY

HERD OF BUFFALO

There is a single, fearless leader in a buffalo herd, and all the other buffalo follow. Buffalo followership is incredible, and their loyalty is unquestioned, but their adaptability and resilience are weak. The buffalo depend on one leader so strongly that the loss of that leader leaves them vulnerable. Early settlers of the west would take out the lead buffalo first because, without their leader, the rest of the herd just stood around. The herd would be slaughtered when the lead buffalo was killed because they did not know how to lead or make decisions.

FLOCK OF GEESE

I have always enjoyed watching geese fly south for the winter. They fly in their "V" formation with noteworthy alignment toward warmer weather. The geese even take turns bearing the burden of flying in the lead position. To me, geese represent a group of responsible, committed, and interdependent workers. The geese framework of collaboration represents the journey we are on at Century Fence to ultimately fly in a "V" formation every single day.

The journey from a herd of buffalo to a flock of geese is the journey we have embarked on since my transition to president. It's certainly a rocky road, but it's a road worth traveling. It is a journey of unleashing everyone's gifts; it is an opportunity for all to fly and share and collaborate as we travel to our destination.

CHAPTER TWELVE

Before I became president, our business was redlining. Yes, we were stringing record years together for over eight years, but at what expense? Not long ago, one of our top superintendents died from a heart attack. Another needed to take time off to deal with depression and anxiety. Mental health resources had become an increasing request from employees.

This is the opposite of human flourishing. The income statement looks good, but at what cost?

The culture of the business was structured around squeezing instead of building. The business was fortunate to have loyal teammates throughout the organization. We are rebooting the culture and operations toward building people up and cultivating the soil for the team to flourish and not redline. If machines should not redline, neither should people!

PEOPLE MOMENTUM

Peter Drucker stresses in *The Effective Executive* that a leader must find ways to bring out the best in the people. There's no such thing as a perfect employee. As Robert Greenleaf points out in his book *Servant as Leader,* "Acceptance of the person... requires a tolerance of imperfection. Anybody could lead perfect people." The concept of "people momentum" puts the responsibility on the leader of an organization to understand how your people are wired and appreciate the experiences they have to leverage to help the company strive closer toward the vision. Put them in the right seat on the bus, as Jim Collins would phrase it.

The concept of momentum provides granularity and tangibility to make meaningful progress. It seems to only be a concept for a company that truly puts its people first because it requires a true passion to understand your people.

I disagree with a fixed mindset model that encourages immediately writing people off if they don't perform well. Things are rarely that black and white. It's important to take the onus as a leadership team to make sure we are clear and provide the environment for flourishing.

After sitting through about seven years of formal reviews, I always feel the importance of trust and the significance of asking the right questions. Performance reviews of the past were very nonchalant and without strategy, lacking structure and preparation. Not to mention, the reviews oftentimes did not involve the direct reports.

We are keeping in place the legacy aspect of every teammate providing a formal opportunity to sit down for an extended period to discuss their experiences and ideas. Giving people special attention and consideration is an instrumental aspect of the culture we are seeking to build.

Today, our performance reviews lean toward seeking deeper understanding and building trust. We also discuss how the individual can contribute to enhancing the culture of the team with clear language around the accepted behaviors (i.e., our company values).

Strengthening a company's teams enhances retention and output for the larger organization. People depending on people is the essence of a team. At the core of our human experience, we are seeking a sense of belonging. Century Fence is achieving that in the years to come!

PERFORMANCE BONUSES AND BEHAVIOR

I was first exposed to our company's bonus allocation process in my second to last year as vice president. I had spent my first several years just receiving bonuses with no understanding of how the dollar amount was decided upon. It fostered significant buzz within the company. The bonus process fit the previous leadership's culture but will not fit well for the future with a focus on transparency, collaboration, and working together. After a year of hard work, being handed a check across the table for work you did over twelve months can be a bit anti-climactic.

We were a company that relied heavily on bonuses to reduce overhead on salaries, so naturally, bonuses were always on everyone's minds; because of that, and the fact that they were decided by one individual, it unintentionally led to a political environment.

Once I became involved in the bonus allocation process myself,

I realized I had not appreciated how much thought went into the bonuses. Many variables were taken into consideration: compensation, perception of performance, trajectory in the company, and more. There were a lot of moving parts, but no one on the receiving end could appreciate that because all that was seen was the final number, the check.

One of the great opportunities I discovered when I became president was that because we did not have a formal performance review process, I did not need to unwind anything. Instead, we could simply put productive processes into place.

Motivational speaker Marcus Buckingham phrased it so eloquently in his book *Nine Lies About Work* when he said, "Human beings can never be trained to reliably rate other human beings... [This] reveals far more of the rater than it does of the person being rated." He continues, "Your rating of a team member on something called 'performance' is unreliable, because your definition of performance is unique to you."

This is profound and once again points those in leadership positions toward a place of reflective humility. The first step to revamping a performance process is coming to terms with one's inability to accurately judge. I doubt most leaders in most companies would be willing to admit and come to terms with this reality. That is their loss. Those companies will trudge along in a culture of ego.

Buckingham also suggests a solution: "Although we are not reliable raters of others, people can reliably rate their own experience." He also states, "Reliable doesn't mean accurate. Reliable means something doesn't fluctuate randomly."

Focus on rating your *own* experience with the individual first, and see where that takes you.

I find these questions to be helpful in structuring bonuses based upon the answers of the direct report as they share their perceptions of individuals:

- **Effectiveness:** Do you turn to this team member when you want extraordinary results?
- **Teamwork:** Do you choose to work with this team member as much as you possibly can?
- **Potential and Intent:** Would you promote this person today if you could?
- **Concerns:** Do you think this person has a performance problem that you need to address immediately?

These questions focus on the leader's own feelings and intentions. This does not give a complete picture, but it does provide a reliable view of the leader's perception.

To quote Buckingham on the topic one last time, a bonus is "the reaction of [the] team leader to you." It is not reflective of some deeper truth or value. It simply is a reflection of the leader's feeling and what the leader would do in the future.

This is how bonuses should be treated and, this way, they can be much more effective. We are transitioning compensation toward higher salaries and base wages to provide for the day-to-day living of our people and their families. Providing extraordinarily heavy bonuses and light salaries is a good structure for a business but creates anxiety for the team. I have found heavy performance bonuses create unnecessary politics and even a lack of safety because of so much anxiety around one day defining a family's financial well-being.

THE GREAT RESIGNATION

It was very difficult to fill positions and to keep them filled. I received a resignation letter from a Gen Z employee we had invested significant time into. Instead of blaming that person for not being a good fit, I reflected on what in the culture was not a good fit. Was there something Century Fence needed to systemically change?

The culture the Gen Z employee was seeking:

- **Autonomy of time:** the ability to arrive between 7:00 a.m. and 8:00 a.m. and leave between 3:30 p.m. and 5:30 p.m.
- **Fun:** leave early on Fridays and have offsite happy hours (belonging)
- **Team atmosphere:** he felt isolated in the corner we put him in and wanted to feel, on a daily basis, a sense of collaboration

At the time, we fell short in all three categories. I didn't need to judge his statements. It was simply true: we did not check the boxes he wanted from an employer.

Now that I'm president, I have been working to bend our company's culture toward autonomy, collaboration, and fun. We need to be able to strike a balance between attaining results and infusing meaning and fun into the daily tasks.

That employee's resignation was symbolic of a weakness in

our company culture and an opportunity for improvement in the years to come. This is one anecdotal example, but it is pervasive throughout the business community. The upcoming workforce has systemically different expectations, and business leaders must adapt. At Century, we are in construction, so we don't have the luxury of the flexibility of other industries, but we can find a balance in the years to come.

IT'S NOT ALL ABOUT THE MONEY

"A good compensation program is not a substitute for recognition. Compensation and recognition address different human needs."
—JIM CANFIELD AND KRAIG KRAMERS

Century Fence offers a lucrative monetary package through performance bonuses. Yes, in recent years, the construction industry as a whole has struggled to acquire and hold onto quality workers. Even so, great people find great companies. I'm optimistic that "The Great Resignation" offers every company an opportunity to reflect and build a great team. It is an opportunity to build an institution that prospects see as a place to chase dreams.

Just writing a check to employees is not enough. I think that is lazy and misses an opportunity to truly connect with people. Cultivating an environment for people to attain greatness needs to be the goal.

The difference between Wikipedia and Microsoft Encarta is a fascinating case study of proving money is not a silver bullet. Microsoft was seeking to build a platform for answers to all sorts of facts. Microsoft invested significant sums of money and paid the people building Encarta top dollar. By contrast, Wikipedia was operated by a group of volunteers committed to a journey of building something great. A vision was clear, and the Wikipedia team all rowed in the same direction.

Wikipedia is still around. Microsoft Encarta isn't.

I'm on a journey to build an institution that goes beyond compensation and specializes in recognition. I want our company to provide people with the intrinsic, human need for affirmation and an irreplaceable sense of belonging. Providing meaningful work is a necessity and a requirement by the workforce now as we adapt in the era of "The Great Resignation."

HARRY TRUMAN—BLUEPRINT FOR THE FIRST DAY AS PRESIDENT

Franklin Roosevelt was a seasoned statesman with over twelve years in the US presidential seat. He understood the nuances of diplomacy and was a charismatic leader pushing the Allied forces toward a victory against the Nazis. When he passed away during his fourth term, it fell to Harry Truman to fill the nation's first chair.

Unlike Roosevelt, Truman came from humble beginnings. He hadn't grown up around the concept of becoming president as Roosevelt had. At the age of sixty-one, Truman was thrown into the presidency with zero preparation or guidance from Roosevelt.

The first thing Truman did was walk from the White House to

Capitol Hill. There, he had an informal lunch with seventeen members of the Senate. There's often tension between the legislative and executive branches of government. Roosevelt was infamous for the tension that existed between himself and the Senate. Truman did not allow his promotion to president to prevent him from building relationships and changing the dynamics between the two branches of government.

At this lunch, Truman encouraged the senators to call him "Harry" and told them he *needed their help.* He shared his vulnerability and stressed he would not be able to lead alone. Truman did not allow his ego to get in the way of his mission to be a steward of the United States.

Truman made his first big speech to the American people following this lunch with the senators. He used the same speech writer as Roosevelt but ended his speech to the American people with a prayer:

> Give therefore Thy servant an understanding heart to judge Thy people, that I may discern between good and bad; for who is able to judge this Thy so great a people? I ask only to be a good and faithful servant of my lord and my people.

Truman's priority was seeking wisdom between good and bad while also being a servant to the people. Truman was building a foundation of trust, and he never tried to be someone he wasn't. He was not trying to be a charismatic Roosevelt. He was leaning into his roots as a Missouri farm boy—his upbringing was that of an industrious and honest farmer. He wanted to keep things simple and surround himself with a team willing to bring their best to the table.

Truman did not want to build a buffalo herd model of one genius and a thousand helpers. He sought to bring out the best in his coworkers. On his first day as president, Truman was already hard at work building trust with his coworkers in government and, most importantly, the American people.

Truman's first day should serve as a blueprint for all leaders stepping into the role. One can never be fully prepared, and it's okay to admit it. Truman had to lead the Allied forces to the finish line with no reputation to leverage with the American people. He came to the people with vulnerability, humility, and with a heart seeking to *serve*.

PEOPLE-BUILDING OR PEOPLE-USING

Are employees resources or are they partners?

Does the company language lean toward "we" or does it lean toward "*them* and *us*"?

Does the leadership team feel optimistic about their workforce, or does the leadership team assume employees are lazy and out to extract value?

As a 105-year-old business, we have an incredible opportunity to evolve the culture and the approach of how the leadership team partners with the workforce of the twenty-first century.

A company cannot truly provide an opportunity for human flourishing until the leadership team becomes a people-building organization. Employees cannot feel autonomous until they feel trusted. Managers in a people-using organization want the resources to trust while not being willing to trust the resources.

The approach of people-building solidifies a culture of autonomy, which ultimately leads to everyone on the team gaining mastery in their respective roles. Mastery leads to more production and efficiency, thus leading to a more successful organization.

How does a company go from people-using to people-building?

I think it first starts with the leadership team. As an owner of the company and president, I want to build the leadership team up. I want the leadership team to know my primary objective in the business is to serve them.

My grandfather is from a different generation and was very forward-thinking for his time in how he financially rewarded our team. The president who preceded me was also from a very different generation as well and thrived with the version of the company's framework and culture. So, I was wary about shaking the apple cart by implementing new changes for the team during my first seven years in the business when it was not my time to lead.

I planned to invest heavily in the leadership team so Century, as a company, could truly put people first. On this topic, Robert Greenleaf, servant-leader guru, states: "An institution starts on a course toward people-building with leadership that has a firmly established context of people first." While I was in the second chair preparing for my transition to president, I was building a strategic plan, articulating the importance of putting people first and building a foundation of values around the concept of caring for our people.

I continue to seek the right balance of respecting and appreciating the past while also deepening my understanding of how to lay the groundwork for the future. The company has had tremendous success leading into my transition to president, and I see the only way to continue the momentum is to unlock the potential of the team through the empowerment of the most important aspect of the company, our people.

It's an exciting time to be in a position to serve. At the end of my transition out of the second chair, I had the opportunity to form our first strategic plan, and I formalized the vision and values of the company.

People come first.

IT'S NOT ABOUT THE FENCES (OR THE PAVEMENT MARKING)…

Everyone thinks we're in the business of fences and pavement marking.

But that isn't exactly accurate.

We're in the business of people.

We happen to be a contractor.

PART FOUR

WITH FAMILY

CHAPTER THIRTEEN

FAMILY BUSINESS IS AN INFINITE GAME

"A business that makes nothing but money is a poor kind of business."

—HENRY FORD

There is no finish line in business. The game is to stay in the game. Success is found in transcending generations and bolstering the business so it can adapt and change with the times. The most beautiful aspects of family business come from putting relations above profit. Finding and fostering courageous patience in the infinite game of business is mission critical in family business.

Unfortunately, lots of business advice is offered in the spirit of a finite game with a finite mindset. An infinite mindset is required to play an infinite game like owning and operating a family business. An infinite mindset is that of stewardship with a focus on long-term value. A finite mindset is focused on "What about me?" On the contrary, an infinite mindset leaves a person asking: "What about *us*?"

In order for a family business to succeed, it is critical that we realize we are playing an infinite game. Maintaining a finite mindset leads to a lack of trust and many missed opportunities. The infinite game requires a cultivation of relationships.

True, long-lasting stewardship is about transcending generations. Most companies do not make it beyond three generations. Why? Because a generation with a finite mindset that was not playing the right game inadvertently leads the business into short-term. Ultimately, that results in extinction.

STEWARDSHIP

"There is joy in self-forgetfulness... So I try to make the light in others' eyes my sun, the music in others' ears my symphony, the smile on others' lips my happiness."

—HELLEN KELLER

Living a life of service moves the focus from the self and repositions it toward others, allowing such a steward to enjoy a life of relations, commitment, and meaning. As Viktor Frankl stated, "The door to happiness opens outward."

"Stewardship" has become my favorite word since joining the family business. The richness found in service is profound. The act of stewardship prevents the seeds of ego from taking root and growing into weeds. The act of service provides sustainable fulfillment to carry on the challenging journey of keeping a family business thriving.

Without stewardship, the journey becomes an ego-driven venture. I would never have sustained the journey if I were preoccupied with solely looking out for myself. Being a part of a story bigger than myself has made me more resilient, and that resiliency has ultimately made me a better leader. An ego-centric approach to operating a family business makes one vulnerable to pitfalls. An ego-centric approach is like focusing on a tree branch with many snappable twigs. Alternatively, an approach focused on stewardship is like focusing on the *whole tree*: resilient, steady, and stoic.

The battle against our ego is a constant one. I am always mindful of my ego's propensity to try to sprout up during my decision-making process. I am always trying to prune my ego, so it does not take over. By operating from an intentional place of stewardship, *all* of our branches have the space to grow flowers.

Family businesses require stewardship. A family business is a union. This brings Abraham Lincoln to mind. Lincoln walked the path of keeping the country together during a bloody war of disagreement. He was willing and able to bear the burden of the war. In short, Lincoln was a steward of the union.

Lincoln was also a guru of self-education. He was a lifelong learner. As a young congressman, his leadership grew as he witnessed a trainwreck of leadership under President Polk and the Mexican War. Through his experience as a congressman, he became a nuanced, humble leader and eventually was responsible for navigating the country through the dark days of the Civil War.

William Lee Miller's biography on President Lincoln, *Lincoln's Virtues*, describes Lincoln's feelings on the matter:

The Mexican Government not only refused to receive him or listen to his propositions, but after a long-continued series of menaces, have at last invaded our territory and shed the blood of our fellow citizens on our own soil.

Polk was a self-righteous man defending his actions. He declared America to be in the right and Mexico to be completely in the wrong. Polk was pursuing his agenda with blinders on. Ego was clearly front and center in the war agenda.

As congressman, Lincoln attacked Polk on many fronts for what he perceived as an unjustifiable war:

Let him answer, fully fairly, and candidly. Let him answer with facts, and not with arguments....If the president cannot or will not give the desired answers...that he is deeply conscious of being in the wrong—that he feels the blood of this war.

Lincoln was a lifelong learner. He grew out of issuing personal attacks on others and internalized the damage an egotistical first-chair leader can create with ego at the forefront.

Lincoln's arguments as a congressman were personal, emotional, and blunt. He approached his argument against President Polk in a binary "yes/no" format, automatically putting Polk and his constituents on the defensive. These personal attacks created tension, making a discussion to discover truth and discover the right path forward next to impossible. The conversation became about egos rather than the issue at hand.

In other words, they were playing the blame game.

Lincoln internalized a completely different approach as president than Polk had. He took the approach of a humble servant. He did not stand on his podium and declare his righteousness. He guided the country through a very dark time and sought to find a path forward for all. That path required a leader who did not point fingers and who could guide a conversation of forgiveness and generosity.

President Polk insisted the other side was altogether to blame for the beginning and the continuance of the war. Lincoln, as Miller's biography went on to say, "would not reiterate the South's guilt; he would recommend amnesty toward the Confederate leaders and generosity to the Southern people."

Being a family steward requires the maturity of Lincoln when he was president. We can find a path forward when we put down our fingers of blame, and we seek a collaborative approach forward. Lincoln learned to marry his level of aspiration with discipline and economy of words to align a shared vision.

UNSPOKEN NEEDS

Every family business has three buckets of needs: money, power, and love.

Money talks. It matters. When the dividend checks stop, the music stops. It is human nature to become accustomed to things and to expect the lifestyle we work for.

When it comes to power, status and ego are ever-present components of our existence on this earth. The stories we tell ourselves and the stories others tell of us are important to the ego.

Finally, there is love. In many ways, love is our legacy. Love is where we find our significance and sense of belonging.

Remember, these needs often go unspoken. A family member may or may not voice the reason they are upset. By understanding the issue, a steward can properly address and begin to resolve conflict.

If a family member wants an increase in a sense of belonging within the family business, then no percentage increase in the dividend distribution will satisfy the issue at hand.

STRUCTURE OF FAMILY BUSINESS

As a steward of a family business, one must understand self-development and organizational development. Unlike other organizations and their structures, when you get involved in a family business, Thanksgiving, Christmas, Easter, and other holidays become informal shareholder meetings. Business and family merge together in an inescapable way. Family business permeates every aspect of your life. Work does not simply stay inside the four walls of your office. For example, you may have otherwise disengaged family members become quite suddenly interested in the bottom line growth of the business at the Thanksgiving dinner table.

When we think about our family business, it's important to keep in mind the evolution of the self and the family system dynamics of generations.

Self

The priorities of a human in life evolve by decade.

Healthy life cycle:

- **Infant/child:** Developing trust in the world
- **Teenager:** Developing a unique identity
- **Twenties:** Starting to think of life more seriously and building a career
- **Thirties:** Establishing voice and authority in one's chosen profession
- **Forties/fifties:** Questioning one's dreams and goals and redefining one's role
- **Sixties:** Reflection and becoming at peace with mentoring

Each stage poses a unique tension which, if not resolved at that time of life, persists into the next stage. We must have awareness of the different stages everyone around us is experiencing. The parent-child relationship can be tenuous and difficult if the parent (in business, the executive—fifties) is struggling and questioning life while the child (twenties) is just starting to show serious interest (like, say, in joining the family business).

Organization

Looking at a relationship between a parent and a child is difficult enough because there are many moving parts. There is an additional layer of complexity, however, and that is the dynamic of the larger family system, depending on how many generations are involved in the business.

Family ownership structures:

1. Controlling Owner (G1)
2. Sibling Partnership (G2)
3. Cousin Consortium (G3+)

Family systems become increasingly more complex from one generation to the next. The Controlling Owner (G1) level is quite simple and may not require communication to make a buck. A Sibling Partnership is feasible without a lot of intentional work because siblings are usually raised with many common values.

Once an organization reaches the Cousin Consortium (G3+) it's a whole new ball game. This is because now, the shareholders are coming from different value systems and have had entirely different experiences growing up. A Cousin Consortium must be appreciated for the complexity and new ideas it brings. The leaders of the organization need to act accordingly by focusing on over-communicating. When a family feels it is over-communicating, the family is probably hitting the mark.

I still am—and perhaps always will be—learning how the dynamics of operations, board, and family council can successfully work together.

1. Operations
2. Board
3. Family Council

A family council offers a platform for the family to have a safe place to entertain casual yet important discussions while keeping the board and operations as a more professional setting.

It's a lot more productive to have a formal platform for family members to share lifestyle, philanthropic, and family hiring dynamics in this type of a space, which is explicitly family.

BUILDING RELATIONS—NOT JUST AT BOARD MEETINGS

That said, it's important for family members to feel like they are part of the family. Only seeing family at a board meeting creates a transactional energy. It's important to schedule time for family outside of family business. Trust and connection need to be fostered in ways that have nothing to do with careers and income.

That's not only a wise business strategy—it's simply the right thing to do.

At the end of our lives, it is those non-business meetings that will have been the most important. The times your family gathered to break bread and to laugh are the meetings that truly matter.

CONTINUITY

Momentum is a tremendous precursor for future success. Strength leads to strength. In this way, a family business has a competitive advantage: continuity. If it does not have continuity, it becomes a liability.

Continuity requires discipline, prudence, and macro patience. Coordinating all parties—between shareholders, board members, management, and employees—can take time.

Zooming out is important in the scheme of a multi-generational business as well. Getting the right people in the right seats, acquiring the right board members, and having the right timing when it comes to succession takes time. A year is a blip in the larger plan.

Continuity is a beautiful journey if one treats it like a shepherd, enjoying the experience rather than racing through it until it is just a blur.

Continuity can have detours, and these detours can be life lessons utilized to galvanize one's potential.

Continuity of business is continuity of family relations.

ORIGINS OF FAMILY BUSINESS CONFLICT

The family business is messy because there's no easy way in or out. Finding alignment requires a massive amount of hard work.

The sources of family business issues fall on a spectrum of estrangement and enmeshment.

- Estrangement: "I'm out"
- Enmeshment: "I'm in"

When it comes to estrangement, letting go and disengaging from business can be extraordinarily difficult and emotional because relations might become strained from the disconnection in business.

As far as enmeshment, families grow faster than business leadership seats. Finding the right seat for each family member can be very difficult. As Teddy Roosevelt so eloquently stated, "Comparison is the thief of joy."

CHAPTER FOURTEEN

MANAGEMENT VS. GOVERNANCE

Growth and succession are completely different skillsets.

The management team and the day-to-day operations of the business are focused on growth. The governance of the business must have the skills to address and ensure succession of the business.

As a member of the next generation, I view the board as an essential aspect of a successful transition. The board oversees the management team. Therefore, they can step in and positively influence inevitable and difficult transitions.

- Management = Growth
- Board = Succession

A board might often devolve into a social club, but it has the potential to be part of the secret sauce that makes a great, enduring company. A good board asks questions before they are needed.

A board provides the opportunity to seek counsel from leaders of organizations you aspire to become.

SUCCESSION PLANNING IS A UNIQUE SKILL

A good management team is good at growing the business. That doesn't necessarily mean they are good at succession. It's a completely different skillset and probably the first attempt for all parties involved.

It's a scary thought to think of an older manager and a newer manager finding their way through a succession plan on their own while simultaneously trying to grow a business. A handoff of responsibilities between an exiting president and an incoming president should strongly consider outside guidance. There is too much at stake in a leadership transition. My transition did not have an outside facilitator explicitly involved, but I would consider it mission critical when my day comes for a transition of leadership.

A board of directors is a phenomenal resource to keep a succession process running smoothly. The board of directors proved vital to continue the succession of my transition into the president role. An outside board can remove emotion from the process taking place between the transitioning leaders. Their involvement can redirect any potential angst or frustration toward the directors rather than the successor and upcoming retiree. When a board is not as involved as it should be, I've found business coaches and CEO peer groups to be outstanding resources. Hiring a business coach proved to be a phenomenal investment for me as it provided me a way to increase my executive skillset as I took on many additional responsibilities. Coaching helped me while I tried to adapt my management style to best fit my strengths in the context of the family business and its existing culture.

The parties involved in the transition could not afford to become aggravated with each other. It's not good for the succession process or the growth of a business. There are so many relationships requiring a prudent handoff:

1. Customer relations
2. Employee relations
3. Vendor relations
4. Shareholder relations

A good handoff makes all relationships feel secure with the future of the company and the leadership capabilities of the up-and-coming leader. During a transition, time becomes a scarcer resource for the successor. For that reason, I've discovered it is important to have a chart with deadlines for relationship handoffs.

Here's an example chart I used during my transition to the first chair:

There are a lot of different tasks I had to take on in my transition. I found it quite easy, though, to understand which aspects of the transition took priority because the relationships are the most important aspect of a transition. I found it helpful to compartmentalize the administrative aspects of my role so becoming president was an easier part of my transition.

As Danny Meyer put it in *Setting the Table*, "Business, like life, is all about how you make people feel. It's that simple, and it's that hard." Making sure people feel cared for and are properly communicated to during a time of transition is of utmost importance.

KING OF THE MOUNTAIN

A transition of leadership offers three very different paths:

1. **King of the Mountain:** The current leader fights off the successor and denies there is a need for a transition.
2. **Walk Down the Mountain:** The current leader is not prepared for the next part of life but relinquishes the leadership seat all the same. This leader may point out some of the traps and the inner workings they've discovered on the way out.
3. **Hang Glide into the Blue Sky:** The current leader brings the successor to the top of the mountain, pointing out landmarks along the way. Once the retiring leader and their successor reach the top, the leader jumps onto a hang glider, soaring as they reach new heights.

The first and second paths are infused with ego. This occurs when the leader has not worked on self-leadership, and so they struggle to let go. A leader who invests in self-leadership has worked the muscles of self-renewal, acceptance, and reinvention.

A business must always be succession planning. The leadership team as a collective—along with each leader as an individual— must always be looking forward.

My experience as a successor with the outgoing president was "King of the Mountain" and a reluctant "Walk Down the Mountain" in the last couple of months of the transition. The good news for those in transition is that as long as the transition is in process there is a lot of growth and opportunity to prepare under one's own control!

Walking down the mountain is not appreciating your God-given gifts and understanding how to be useful in the marketplace and amplify one's skills. Walking down the mountain is accepting retirement as a chapter of relaxation at its best and decay at its worst.

Hang gliding is not what I've experienced in my transition, but I hope to build my career around this concept. I want to build my career and life in such a way that I can empower the generation after me to take on the mountain. When I'm ready, I want to be prepared to take a running jump into the sky with my hang glider—or maybe even a rocket ship!

"Think of an organization like a plant," Simon Sinek writes in his book *The Infinite Game*. "No matter how strong it is, no matter how tall it grows, if it cannot make new seeds, if it is unable to produce new leaders, then its ability to thrive for generations beyond is nil. One of the primary jobs of any leader is to make new leaders!"

Hang gliding is a symbol of a leader who has had their eye on the future. They intentionally build a way to take flight while knowing the next leaders are ready to climb the mountain.

SAFETY IN A TRANSITION

Safety is of the utmost importance in a transition of operational leadership and ownership. It allows everyone on the team to engage in their best work instead of worrying about survival.

The best ways I see to provide safety are to stress the value of continuity, share appreciation, demonstrate an understanding of the legacy, and—in my particular case—help people appreciate that my grandfather was roughly my same age when he became president.

Successors must avoid comparisons at all costs and should never openly criticize the leadership of the past. Everything must remain positive, and it's important to frame conversations with positivity and respect.

We are great and only getting better.

It is important to remember that changing the status quo creates tension.

Transitioning a family business requires constant change: change in leadership, change in technology, change in ownership, change in governance, change in workforce, change in every corner of the business.

As the steward of the business, we need to be okay creating tension. A CEO needs to be comfortable with discomfort. It's okay to have tension when the best interests of the company are at the forefront, and its people are being taken care of.

Creating clarity in a transition also creates tension, but it is healthy. Clarity provides an opportunity to align for the best interests of the business and the family.

FOUNDING VS. INHERITING

Family business is difficult because of the nature of inheriting existing systems built for a previous leader. All generations following the founder are hitching to a trailer of experiences, complexity, expectations, unspoken rules, and a unique culture. For a true steward of a family business, inheritance represents complexity and a need to focus on competency and understanding of the system and all parties involved in the system. Inheriting requires a tremendous capacity for listening and learning what is—before building what will be.

A founder of a company often grows with the company. As the leader grows, the company grows as well. As the founder increases competency, the competency and capacity of the company often grow in tandem. Founding allows for slack in the system because the company is smaller and has less risk while the leader is developing the executive skillset to go along with meeting payroll, delivering the services to the customer, etc.

An inheritor (G2 and beyond) snaps into the role like jumping onto a moving train. There is a lot of risk in a transition of inheriting the role of first chair because the systems are intact and must be understood before building. If the company is successful but has flaws in the system, then it's even more difficult because the cracks are hidden, and not enough tension exists to give the inheritor the impetus to make necessary changes without pushback.

HITCHED TO LEGACY CULTURE

The day I became president, I didn't immediately unhitch our company from the previous leadership culture. To do so would have been a chaotic, jarring mess for everyone involved. Instead, I carried what the role represented for a period of time.

As time has marched on, I hope my leadership style has helped loosen and prepare everyone for a new, empowering era.

It has taken time to untie my leadership from the legacy leadership. It will take even longer to rebrand the corporate support. At the time of my transition, for example, our headquarters was associated as "corporate" in a negative, unapproachable way. My vision for the future is for it to be associated as a place for support. This change is already happening, but it is going to take years.

I still have a trailer of historic leadership hitched to my truck, but I have been slowly unloading the baggage. As a company, we continue to move forward. We persevere and endure, and I try to lead with courage and compassion. Over time, enough legacy items have fallen off the trailer, and I now have the space to place my own items and ideas inside it.

THE LANGUAGE OF LOSS

As the next leader of the family business, I found it critically important to have language for the tremendous transition occurring in all aspects of the business.

The ownership changed, and the management changed. The culture is changing, and our use of technology is changing, too. Priorities are changing, and the workforce is changing.

Change can create a sense of loss of security, even when it's a good thing. Transitions are difficult for this and many other reasons, so it can be helpful to break them down in order to better understand and work with them. All transitions have three distinct phases. The Bridges Model provides important language to articulate what is happening within a transitioning organization:

1. Ending
2. Neutral Zone
3. New Beginning

So, let's break these down.

1. ENDING

When an era is ending, the current leader may feel a significant sense of loss. This can also be true for many other people in the organization who have had a long tenure. Having a leader who has been in their position for decades provides a significant security blanket. Optically, this is also stressful for people, as many of them have only ever received checks with the legacy president's signature. That familiarity is valuable to them.

So, it's accurate to label this part as "Ending." After all, people are experiencing a significant loss. It's important for the next generation to be considerate and to accept that people will be feeling a range of emotions. There will be some who are excited, some who are mad, some who are skeptical, some who are sad, and some who couldn't care less.

2. NEUTRAL ZONE

This is the phase of the transition when the legacy leader finally takes a bow and walks off the stage. This is where innovation and the future begin to form. As the new leader, this is the time to lean in and show concern and care. We want to help all aspects of the business; employees, customers, vendors, and shareholders all need to feel heard and cared for.

Leading with concern and care will bring all stakeholders to a new foundation of trust. This will be the phase of the transition that will require the most attention from the new leader. Successors must be fully in tune and hyper-conscious of the attention this part of the transition requires and the potential it represents.

It is wise to help facilitate many tiny wins in order to help build momentum. This is the time to facilitate conversations about building a new culture.

3. NEW BEGINNING

This marks a time of excitement. This is a time of facilitating and empowering the leadership team. It is during this phase that a company can move forward with momentum, learning, leading, and ultimately leaping into the future.

FAMILY CONVERSATION

A conversation with family can be very different from one with a coworker.

With my grandfather, I'm able to take it deeper. I'm able to share my vision and desire to succeed for the family and to continue his legacy.

I can share with him feelings like, "I've got the desire and the ability. I've got this."

I realized only after I became president that I had undervalued the card I could pull as a next-generation family member. I can speak at a level no one else can. I can speak at the intersection of business and family. This is a very powerful intersection no one else in the business is able to stand in.

COMING BACK TO PATIENCE

Succession requires acceptance from shareholders, leaders, and board members. Most institutions are not living through the process intentionally. It is often a reactionary process. As the successor, it's not always about what is right or what is best.

In a family business transition, there are days (most days) when it is about what *is*.

Learning to deal with less than ideal conditions is another opportunity to lean into patience. It's vital to focus on what we can control rather than focusing on the aspects of the transition we do not have control over as a successor.

In my last year as vice president, I found myself in a difficult spot. I was responsible for the success of the company the following year, when I was to be president, yet I could not take action in the way I felt was necessary to retain the workforce and prepare for the years ahead. The financial success of the company was minimizing the storm clouds I perceived on the horizon. I noticed there would be cultural issues when recruiting the next wave of our workforce. I saw private equity companies purchasing companies to capture market share for the short-term. I saw the existing workforce needing to be recharged and gain new skills.

As successors, we need to find peace in the transition. We need to prevent our insecurities from poisoning things, and we must avoid seeking opportunities to blame and seek out how unjust the process feels. All of the struggles and the lack of guidance serve to strengthen the executive skillset. Courageous patience leads to building strong relationships with family and your team in the company.

CHAPTER FIFTEEN

When the next generation joins, it is with a spirit of hope. It is with a spirit that seeks to bend culture, join something great, and do something good in the world. The next generation burns bright with the flame of hope and is eager to contribute. I joined the family business after experiencing other companies and their various cultures. I was being used and not being cared for or cultivated. I wanted to join a business where I could be part of keeping promises and being true. My flame burned big and bright when I joined my family's business.

Over the seven years I spent in the second chair, I have come to appreciate the fragility of this flame. It can be overwhelming to be part of a family business where many aspects of life come together: mortality, transition, power, and status.

The upcoming generation often receives the brunt of emotions that bubble up during periods of transition. The flame of hope and excitement can dim if it is deprived of oxygen. Artificial harmony is like trapping a candle inside an overturned glass. The flame, once bright and burning, can quickly become extinct. The flame can be diminished with empty promises and a lack of clarity. That's when the work becomes a job rather than a passion. It becomes a paycheck rather than a legacy.

The generation in charge and in control of succession has the responsibility to be proactive and guide the upcoming generation so everyone benefits and succeeds. The more a leader holds on to their status and power, the less oxygen there is to fan the flames of the next generation. I hope to be a leader who inspires the next generation. I hope to proactively fan the flames when it is my turn to transition.

GRANDFATHER AND GRANDSON WITH THE LAWYERS

My grandfather and I were in a meeting with our family attorney near the end of the transition of me becoming president. We were discussing some important estate and succession decisions for the family and the business. My grandfather stated with a smile and pride to the attorneys in the room:

> I'm not concerned about control [of the company] if I have my grandson by my side!

This was a very meaningful moment because it was an authentic, genuine statement where both of us knew we are in it for the infinite game of transition and not the myopic moment of money. My grandfather has held the torch for over six decades as the leader of the family business and we have built a wonderful relationship along the succession journey.

The trust and sentiment my grandfather shared has made the challenges and struggles to get to the first chair worth it. I will

cherish his trust and certainly will make sure to continue to
make him proud.

ARE YOU READY?

Regardless of the cohesive nature (or lack thereof) of a transition, there are steps to take to make sure you are ready for the first chair role. Here is the operational checklist I used to get ready:

- Cultivate relationships and trust with your team by listening.
- Understand the current leader's daily, weekly, monthly, quarterly, and annual tasks.
- Study and intimately understand the systems and processes throughout the organization.
- Foster a network of business owners, CEOs, presidents, and thought leaders.
- Invest heavily in books.
- Write out your playbook for improving the health of your organization the moment you land in the first chair.
- Remain patient and remember that how you react and follow during the transition sets the culture for how the team will react under your leadership.

YOU ARE NOT ALONE

Family business is messy. It is a wondrous, beautiful, and explosive combination of love, legacy, money, power, ego, mortality, and competition, all intertwined.

There have been days when I have felt no one understands me or what the future requires. Sometimes, it has felt like no one understands or appreciates how I am trying to live in the present culture while seeking to plant seeds for a flourishing future.

Pressure is a privilege. It would be terribly boring to go into a cubicle every day with no demands and no pace or expectations. Hard work is rewarding in and of itself. It is an honor and an amazing opportunity to reframe the challenges as opportunities to grow and become a stronger, better person.

It is a learning experience to take on a leadership role with over one hundred families expecting operations to run smoothly, a board of directors expecting to increase shareholder value, and a family looking forward to continued financial success.

A steward of a family business provides a richness to life well beyond money. It is a journey to seek to be a family builder AND a business builder. There are moments that have been incredibly frustrating. However, this is a journey of being a good person and making the world a better place. It's a journey of putting relations above profits. It's about building and bringing art to an industrialist society. It's about bringing faith and the teachings of Sunday into Monday.

Those of us on this fruitful journey of stewarding businesses to transcend generations must never forget: we are not alone. We are traveling up a mountain with dips, but the journey is worth pursuing because we become better people in the process. You are not alone. You are never alone.

As we go on this journey of family business and inevitably travel into a dark valley, it's important to remember the words of Anthony de Mello: "Don't change. Don't change. Don't change. I love you just the way you are." As the leaders of our family, our business, and our community, we must find contentment in our hearts that we are *enough* regardless of the external outcomes.

This journey has days of blue skies and days of rain. All days include the sun, even if you can't see it.

ACKNOWLEDGMENTS

I need to thank first and foremost "G-Dad" (Tony Bryant) and Grandma Andrea (Andrea Bryant), for making this journey possible to join Century Fence. It is truly an honor to be a part of the family business. Most importantly, the deepening of our relationship over the past several years is what I cherish most.

None of this would be possible without the incredible support of my beautiful wife, Chelsea. She has supported my journey in the family business agreeing to move to Wisconsin without knowing anyone and restarting her master's program from scratch to allow me the opportunity. She has been my rock throughout the succession journey to becoming president. She is the foundation of the existence of this book. I would be a wandering man without her guidance and fluorescent energy. She pushes me every day to be the best version of myself.

The biggest inspiration for this book and my newfound obsession for human flourishing is all thanks to my adorable and vibrant daughter Elizabeth Jane ("EJ"). Thank you for being my inspiration to pushing this book to the finish line. Thank you, EJ, for giving me the unquenchable desire to be helpful in contributing to a better future for the next generation.

I would like to thank my dad, Steve Powell, for showing me throughout my childhood his daily actions of what being a master of one's craft and being a loving family man looks like. You struck the balance of these two mission critical roles with flawless ease.

I must thank Jane and Kurt Gloeckner, for always showing me their support and love. You opened your home to me even when I was a seventeen-year-old wearing a tank top with camo shorts. Their love has been so deep and unconditional for over fifteen years.

I would like to thank my extended family, specifically my aunts, for your support and trust in the work I have put into OUR family business. Thank you for your support and trust!

Thank you, Coach Ben D'Alessandro, for being such an integral part of my formation in becoming a young Christian man. You were instrumental in helping me understand the direct relationship between effort and greatness. Thank you for helping me understand that one must practice according to their aspirations.

I would like to thank five mentors in particular who provided grounded and principled counsel during my seven-year journey to becoming president: Mark Vincent, Phil Bergey, Eric Jorgensen, Dick Pieper, and Karl Williams. My journey thus far would not have been nearly as rich, fulfilling, or successful without their counsel. My eyes have been opened through conversation with these incredible men that business is a medium to transform the lives of those you serve.

I must thank the Century Fence team! Great businesses have great people. Thank you for allowing me to walk alongside you as we build an organization of flourishing!

I have so many other people to thank. I have built so many wonderful friendships and relationships during this journey—thanks you for your support!

I feel like a turtle on a fence post. I did not get here on my own. I have been lifted throughout my life by incredible love. I have been blessed with so many loving relationships to be able to serve from a full cup.